Tax Theory Applied to the Digital Economy: A Proposal for a Digital Data Tax and a Global Internet Tax Agency

Tax Theory Applied to the Digital Economy: A Proposal for a Digital Data Tax and a Global Internet Tax Agency

Cristian Óliver Lucas-Mas and Raúl Félix Junquera-Varela

 **WORLD BANK GROUP**

Contents

Boxes

Figures

Tables

Foreword

Digitalization affects the entire global economy. The impact of this new technological wave can neither be ring-fenced to specific sectors of the economy nor be circumscribed to specific countries or regions. As a consequence, the use of new digital technology has not only transformed traditional business models but has also enabled the appearance of new digital-based business models that pose challenges to how economies have traditionally been taxed. A major breakthrough has been the ability to conduct business activities in a territory without having a physical presence there; in addition, the increasing reliance on intangibles has made it more difficult to differentiate value across different business functions, risks, and assets.

Altogether, digitalization has contributed to a new borderless world economy, which, in turn, has brought to the fore how increased world trade affects the ability of country governments to tax economic activities to fund public priorities. Increased international digital trade has put in check established tax rules, and they need to be updated. In the absence of an international digital tax system and a global tax authority, the digital debate demands multilateral cooperation mechanisms and compromise from all parties involved—mainly from digital producer and consumer countries but also from multinational corporations in the digital services sector. Unless a coordinated global solution is reached, a proliferation of unilateral tax measures could fuel trade wars and negatively affect investment decisions, both cross-border and domestically.

The 2015 Addis Ababa Action Agenda on Financing for Development emphasized "the importance of inclusive cooperation and dialogue among national tax authorities on international tax matters" to support achievement of the Sustainable Development Goals. This effort is especially relevant in the midst of the COVID-19 pandemic crisis, when countries are facing an unprecedented fiscal deficit and online commerce is soaring worldwide. Taxation of the digital economy could be an important measure for governments to generate new fiscal space and increase tax revenues. However, taxing the digital economy is particularly challenging in countries with low tax administration capacity. Special attention should be given to the tax administration dimension, which is largely dismissed by most international tax practitioners. Digital technology has the potential to transform tax administration and its interaction with taxpayers.

The World Bank recognizes that the digital economy, as a driver of growth and innovation, can help to accelerate the achievement of the World Bank Group's twin goals. For example, the World Bank Group Digital Economy for Africa (DE4A) flagship initiative, together with other development partners and sector stakeholders, supports the transformation strategy for Africa that has been prepared by the African Union: to achieve the All Africa Digital Transformation vision. But digitalization must also ensure, as envisioned in the Addis Ababa Action Agenda, that "all companies, including multinationals, pay taxes to the governments of countries where economic activity occurs and value is created, in accordance with national and international laws and policies." To this end, the Macroeconomics, Trade, and Investment (MTI) Global Practice leads the World Bank Group's dialogue and engagement with clients in macroeconomics, fiscal policy, and trade and conducts cutting-edge and innovative research in the area of taxation of the digital economy. This publication is a product of the Global Tax Program (GTP) in the Fiscal Policy and Sustainable Growth Unit (FPSG).

The book analyzes the distinctive features of the digital economy and their tax impact. After identifying the tax-disruptive aspects of digital business models, the authors review existing tax initiatives in light of traditional tax theory principles and discuss a comprehensive solution that is mindful of the foundations of tax theory. In this vein, the book proposes establishing a digital data tax (DDT) that could become a significant source of tax revenues for market jurisdictions while respecting tax theory principles. It also proposes creating a new global internet tax agency (GITA) under the auspices of the United Nations that would provide technical assistance and help to solve disputes around taxing the digital economy.

This is a technical piece, with a fresh view that contributes new ideas and original thinking to a thorny subject. The authors, well known by academics and development professionals, propose a new paradigm for digital taxation—one that would continue to benefit from a collaborative and open intellectual debate. I hope that the contents of this book will foster additional debate among all stakeholders and help to advance the digital taxation agenda.

Marcello Estevão
Global Director, Macroeconomics, Trade, and Investment
World Bank Group

Preface

The idea of writing this book came up in June 2019 while we were having dinner in Riyadh, where both of us were working. We were talking about the interest spurred by direct taxation of the digital economy and the scope and tax implications of the initiatives under debate to address the related tax challenges and respond to the G-20 mandate to reach a global and consensus-based solution during Saudi Arabia's 2020 G-20 presidency. During our discussion, we realized that unilateral tax measures and tax proposals had overlooked the importance of traditional tax theory principles, which must guide tax policy design and tax administration decisions. Moreover, the boundaries of what constituted the digital economy were becoming blurred, and the scope of work was shifting its focus away from the original G-20 mandate. Therefore, we decided to analyze the distinctive features of the digital economy and their tax impact and, once we had identified the tax-disruptive aspects, to review existing tax initiatives in light of traditional tax theory principles. We would try to contribute a comprehensive proposal that would be mindful of tax theory foundations and that would overcome the shortcomings previously identified during the critical analysis. This book is the outcome of that effort, and the digital taxation debate is still ongoing.

Our objective was to explain in plain language difficult technical concepts, going back to basics without preconceived ideas, and analyzing this new reality from a fresh and unbiased perspective. Our goal was to make a meaningful contribution to the digital taxation debate in a way that our message could reach all audiences, not only tax experts and policy makers, but also nontax government officials, internet users, online business operators, tax students, and even the general public, since all of them will be affected, directly or indirectly, by the solution finally reached, if any. Taxpayers need to understand why they pay taxes and what they get in return for such taxes. When they are not provided with a logical explanation and are pushed to endure an abusive tax burden, even incurring double taxation, as digital multinationals are expected to do, then they lose confidence in the tax system and look for alternative ways to find tax justice. With our work, we aim to find a solution that can be understood by anyone and can be embraced and supported by the global internet user and business community. Such global support is essential to achieving tax compliance and fostering multilateral tax cooperation. Finally, we have been privileged to have world-class, renowned tax experts review our work. They have made very valuable contributions that have improved our analysis and proposal; their comments have been incorporated in the text and notes.

Acknowledgments

This book is a product of the Global Tax Team in the Equitable Growth, Finance, and Institutions Vice Presidency. It draws on a range of the World Bank's operational engagements in the areas of tax policy and administration.

The authors are very grateful to Richard Bird, Stephen Shay, Rick Krever, Richard Ainsworth, Eric Zolt, Daniel Alvarez, and Victor Thuronyi for insightful comments, valuable contributions, and noteworthy technical advice.

They are also appreciative of the comments and observations of peer reviewers Reuven Avi-Yonah, El Hadji Dialigue Ba, Tuan Minh Le, and Jeffrey Owens.

They thank Salma Lemkhente for providing assistance in reviewing the research literature and for sharing her extensive knowledge throughout the drafting process, Ana Cebreiro for giving helpful guidance and technical support, Paola Arce for contributing useful visualizations, and Yesica Morales for providing timely operational support.

They commend the outstanding and professional work of the entire team of the World Bank Publishing Program under the excellent coordination of Mark McClure, with special recognition to Elizabeth Forsyth for making significant and valuable editorial contributions.

The authors also thank Marcello Estevão, William Maloney, and Chiara Bronchi for overall management and direction.

About the Authors

Raúl Félix Junquera-Varela is global lead on domestic revenue mobilization and lead tax specialist in the Fiscal Policy and Sustainable Growth Unit, Macroeconomics, Trade, and Investment Global Practice, of the World Bank. He has more than 30 years of experience in public sector reform, with a particular focus on tax administration and customs. He held senior positions at the Spanish Revenue Agency from 1984 to 1998, including as director of a regional Tax and Customs Office and senior national tax auditor in the Large Taxpayer Office. He headed the Spanish Diplomatic Mission at the Inter-American Centre of Tax Administration and served as public finance counselor to the Spanish Embassy in Panama from 1998 until 2004. In 2005, he joined the International Monetary Fund as technical assistance adviser in the Revenue Administration Division of the Fiscal Affairs Department. In 2009, he joined the World Bank as senior public sector specialist in the Public Sector Governance Department. His research interests include institution building and operational reform of revenue administrations, and he has authored numerous publications on these topics. He is an economist, a lawyer, and a certified public accountant. From 1990 until 1992, he was professor of tax law at the University of Oviedo, Spain. From 2005 until 2015, he was professor of the Master of Public Finance program of the Institute for Fiscal Studies of Spain.

Cristian Óliver Lucas-Mas is senior international tax specialist in the Global Tax Team of the World Bank. He has more than 20 years of experience in international taxation as an attorney at law, economist, consultant, researcher, and university professor. He was admitted to practice law in New York and Spain, where he started his career in a leading law firm and later opened his own private legal practice, specializing in international tax planning, transfer pricing, and taxation of corporate reorganizations. In academia, he has held various teaching positions at Harvard University, the University of Barcelona, Pyongyang University of Science and Technology, Toulouse Business School, Pompeu Fabra University, and La Salle University and has published extensively in international tax journals. As consultant, he has worked as a tax policy adviser for the International Monetary Fund and as an adviser for the General Authority of Zakat and Tax of Saudi Arabia. Since 2016, he has worked at the World Bank, where he has provided technical assistance and tax advice to more than 20 countries in the areas of transfer pricing, base erosion and profit shifting (BEPS), advanced pricing agreements, permanent establishments, interest deductibility, harmful tax practices, tax sanctions, tax reform, and digital economy. He holds a PhD in tax law and public finance from the University of Barcelona, a master of laws (LLM) from Harvard Law School, a master of public administration (MPA) from the Harvard John F. Kennedy School of Government, and a master in business administration (MBA) from the Massachusetts Institute of Technology Sloan School of Management, and he is a graduate of the International Tax Program (ITP) from Harvard Law School. In 2000, he received the First Prize of the National Awards for Academic Excellence in Legal Studies from the government of Spain, and in 2007 he was named a public service fellow by the Harvard John F. Kennedy School of Government.

Executive Summary

This book is about the scope of state sovereignty, which entails two exclusive faculties that are reserved for governments only: the power to tax and the power to punish. These powers go together, and each needs the other. Governments levy taxes under the threat of punishment, and the necessary institutional means to punish are funded through taxes. The power to tax encompasses the power of states to obtain resources for public purposes from their citizenry and their territory, which is the basis for residence taxation and source taxation, respectively. However, this power needs to be balanced to ensure fiscal sustainability. Unfortunately, high-income economies are facing an unprecedented fiscal deficit, which the post-COVID-19 crisis will exacerbate. In this context, some countries are coming close to exhausting their fiscal space, especially as to raising residence-based taxes, which are unpopular and have a high political cost.

Hence, they are shifting their revenue strategy toward increasing their source taxing rights at the expense of claiming a portion of the residence taxing rights of other countries (mainly, the United States) over the digital economy. This approach, at first popular among constituents, might eventually backfire on them, since a significant share of the tentative direct tax to be paid by nonresident digital companies probably would be shifted to local customers, who already bear the burden of indirect taxes. On the one hand, remote sellers and digital platforms lacking a physical presence pose challenges for their role and responsibilities in the administration of consumption taxes on digital transactions (registration, collection, remittance, enforcement mechanisms). On the other hand, the digital economy has not altered indirect taxing rights, since the power to tax consumption clearly corresponds to market jurisdictions where customers are located. As a result, there is no additional tax revenue to gain for those countries.

Therefore, the digital debate focuses on direct taxation and the creation of new taxing rights arising from the tax claims of market jurisdictions on income obtained by foreign digital suppliers conducting business therein without any physical presence (digital services taxes, Amount A of the Unified Approach of the Organisation for Economic Co-operation and Development [OECD]); these tax claims are the focus of this book. Nonetheless, the digital debate is just the first step toward a much more ambitious plan aimed at increasing source taxing rights even more: by extending newly created taxing rights beyond the digital economy, so as to cover consumer-facing businesses as well, and by allocating fixed returns for certain baseline marketing and distribution activities taking place in market jurisdictions (Amount B of the Unified Approach).

In theory, increasing source taxation would benefit market jurisdictions, especially low- and middle-income countries; in practice, only high-income countries with high tax administration capacity would be able to implement the new rules and to increase their tax revenues. Many such high-income countries are facing rampant fiscal deficits and are unable to increase fiscal debt due to strict fiscal discipline. They are aiming to balance their accounts by sharing in the profits of foreign companies. However, they seek to do so without contributing to funding the ecosystem needed for those businesses to blossom or bearing any losses from the failed cases.

Interestingly enough, this digital clash of national interests is not between rich countries and low- and middle-income countries; instead, it is between high-income economies that invested in technological innovation and high-income economies that neglected the internet as a game-changing technology that could overcome the physical limitations of trade and taxation. Now, after decades and billions invested by the former (countries of residence of digital companies), the latter (market jurisdictions) want to join in the investment return at any (noneconomic) cost, even if that requires dismantling the world tax order.

In brief, it all comes down to widely differing public expenditure priorities. For decades, some countries have invested in welfare policies and social safety net mechanisms (public health, public pensions, public education), while other countries have focused on developing their industrial and business capacities via research and development programs and tax incentives to support technological innovation. Nowadays, welfare countries struggle to fund their public social expenditure programs and turn to those less socially oriented economies, widely criticized even as we speak, to share in the proceeds of their industrial and technological business base. Obviously, countries in the latter group are not willing to surrender or share their tax bases voluntarily, and the outcome of any possible negotiation would be to the detriment of their national economic interests and the efforts and sacrifices endured by their populations.

Therefore, it is hard to imagine a scenario where all countries may reach a consensus, since their interests are completely opposite, and unilateral tax measures have already started proliferating (digital services taxes, equalization levies). In this regard, any measure is unilateral, not only when it is adopted by one country, but also when it is not adopted by all countries. Even if a large group of jurisdictions (Inclusive Framework members) were to agree on a solution, it would still create the same adverse consequences as a unilateral measure in relation to nonparticipating countries, some of which would be relevant economies (China, United States) that would surely apply defensive measures (tariffs) to counteract the negative effects.

The digital debate is just the tip of the iceberg that is heading toward the current international tax order, and the only way to avoid a clash is to reach a compromise. So, when the G-20 issued a mandate to address the tax challenges arising from the digitalization of the economy, what it really meant was to agree on how to increase source income taxing rights and to use the digital debate as a pilot project. In fact, the references made in this book to the G-20 mandate are to be interpreted exclusively as evidence of the disconnect between the scope of the verbatim digital mandate and the work and proposals of the OECD/G20 Inclusive Framework on Base Erosion and Profit Shifting (BEPS). Indeed, considerations of political neutrality and inclusiveness should at all times guide not only the digital debate, but any debate conducive to reforming the international tax order substantially in a manner that is not aligned with traditional tax theory principles, as is creating new source taxing rights in the absence of a physical presence in the market jurisdiction.

The fundamental question is, on what basis should remote sellers be taxed by market jurisdictions? In other words, what do market jurisdictions provide remote sellers that may possibly justify source income taxation and to what extent? To answer this question, it is necessary to understand that traditional tax theory principles exist for a reason; they are not random ideas that can be applied or disregarded arbitrarily. Tax principles encapsulate the lessons learned throughout the history of tax practice, and it is not an easy task to innovate and to create new arguments that may support the creation of new source taxing rights in the absence of clear and verifiable benefits from the governments of market jurisdictions in return for the obligation to pay a new tax. Markets are people, so unless buyers are deemed to belong to governments, it is hard to explain why market jurisdictions should be entitled to a share of the income obtained from sales in the market territory by remote sellers without a physical presence therein. To put it in even simpler terms: what role do the governments of market countries play in the creation and development of nonresident companies that operate remotely in their territories? In any business venture, to share in gains, you must also take losses; the opposite is not only unfair, but also, most importantly, economically inefficient.

In this book, we have analyzed the validity of the tax claims of market jurisdictions from a technical perspective; to do so, we have rigorously followed traditional tax theory principles, which constitute the intellectual framework on which our world tax order is constructed. Hoping to dismantle and tear down the tax foundations on which tax systems worldwide are designed is not only unrealistic, but also very reckless.

As our analysis shows, market jurisdictions' claims to tax the income of remote sellers without a physical presence in the territory are unsubstantiated and not aligned with traditional tax theory principles. Having said that, if market countries still wish to subject such remote sellers to taxation, they should abandon income taxation and move to a license-type tax, which is the idea behind our digital data tax (DDT) proposal. The DDT is a tax that would consist of two components, one of them acting as a toll tax and one acting as a service charge for contracted internet bandwidth (in the global DDT) or for significant digital presence (in national DDTs). Obviously, implementing this proposal would not be exempt from difficulties, especially as it refers to reaching an agreement about the weights of components, the tax rate schedules, and the collection and revenue allocation mechanisms among participant countries. In spite of these difficulties, the DDT could become a significant source of tax revenues for market jurisdictions and a solution that would respect tax theory principles.

The DDT proposal also offers the best compromise out of all current digital taxes and tax initiatives, since it takes into account not only the interests of both source and residence countries but also those of digital multinationals; it represents a trade-off that requires a three-way compromise. For example, the fact that the DDT would not be creditable against residence taxation may prompt multinational enterprises to oppose it, as happens with current digital taxes (digital services taxes, equalization levies). However, if the DDT were fully creditable, then residence jurisdictions would be the ones to fight it, since they would have to absorb the entire DDT, which would erode their tax base, as suggested by current proposals (OECD's Unified Approach). Therefore, we envision a half-way compromise. On the one hand, DDT is not an income tax (because traditional tax theory principles do not support income taxation by source countries without a brick-and-mortar permanent establishment), so residence jurisdictions would not have to give away part of their tax base (via income tax credits). On the other hand, a new taxing right would be recognized in market jurisdictions in the form of a digital license-type tax, which multinational enterprises could deduct as an operating expense against their income taxes back in their residence countries. Consequently, nobody would win, which is the best possible compromise:

- Multinational enterprises would not be subject to a full income tax (or, even worse, to a presumptive turnover-based version of it), which most probably would not be creditable; instead, they would be subject to the DDT, which would be tax deductible.
- Market jurisdictions would get substantial revenues from the DDT, as shown in the case study presented in chapter 7.
- Residence countries would not surrender taxing rights, but they would grant businesses a tax deduction for DDT as an operating cost.

Therefore, the current digital debate derives from political and economic motivations rather than from tax technical considerations. Most, if not all, of the countries currently supporting this change in the status quo of source taxing rights had previously agreed and committed by treaty to give up their taxing rights over income derived by a nonresident in the source country unless the nonresident had a permanent establishment therein. What sudden interests have motivated this change of heart? The only reasonable explanation lies in the fact that such so-called high-income market countries find themselves unable to secure more revenues from their own residents and opt to increase source taxing rights at the expense of eroding residence countries' tax bases or creating double taxation on foreign digital companies. Furthermore, all unilateral digital taxes and proposals to tax the income of foreign digital suppliers operating without a physical presence are based on presumptive taxation (turnover-based digital services taxes, formulaic approach to compute Amount A, withholding of income taxes on e-payments). Presumptive taxation is a tax assessment method that has historically been used only for resident taxpayers. Digital suppliers are foreign based, which creates administrative feasibility issues in relation to nonresident taxpayers.

On a different note, it is interesting that China is not as concerned with the digital debate as the United States is. The only reason is that the majority of jurisdictions claiming new source taxing rights are market countries of US digital multinationals, while the penetration of Chinese digital suppliers in those same countries is almost negligible. Yet China and other industrial countries should be aware that, as already mentioned, digital is just the first step toward a more grandiose plan to increase the scope of source taxing rights beyond the digital economy.

Finally, although we started the tax technical analysis of this book without any preconceived ideas, we found ourselves with a very straightforward conclusion: traditional tax theory does not support the income taxation of remote digital suppliers by source jurisdictions. So, given market countries' need to raise revenue from the digital economy, we decided to explore alternative untaxed digital transactions that could increase their fiscal space. We came up with the international supply of internet bandwidth to access digital markets, which is the digital transaction taxed by our DDT proposal. As a consequence, our proposed DDT does not enter into conflict with other income tax proposals (OECD's Unified Approach), since it aims to tax different transactions from the opposite tax perspective: our DDT proposal taxes foreign digital companies as consumers, while income tax proposals tax them as suppliers.

Abbreviations

AEOI	automatic exchange of information
B2B	business-to-business
B2C	business-to-consumer
B2G	business-to-government
BEPS	base erosion and profit shifting
CFC	controlled foreign corporation
DDT	digital data tax
DSL	digital subscriber line
DST	digital services tax
EU	European Union
G-20	Group of Twenty
GITA	global internet tax agency
GloBE	global base erosion
GST	goods and services tax
ICANN	Internet Corporation for Assigned Names and Numbers
IETF	Internet Engineering Task Force
IP	internet protocol
ISP	internet service provider
ITIN	internet tax identification number
LEI	legal entity identifier
MTC	Multistate Tax Commission
OECD	Organisation for Economic Co-operation and Development
P2P	peer-to-peer
SDP	significant digital presence
TIN	tax identification number
UN	United Nations
VAT	value added tax
WTA	world tax authority

CHAPTER 1

Introduction to Taxing the Digital Economy

What lessons can we draw from the history of international taxation that may be applicable to taxing the digital economy? How different is the digital revolution from previous technological breakthroughs? How does the digital taxation debate align with existing tax norms and proposals? Is the tax notion of permanent establishment obsolete? What is the scope of the G20 mandate and to which extent are current initiatives compliant with it? On what basis do market countries claim new taxing rights over the digital economy? This chapter addresses these questions.

Lessons from the Origins of International Taxation

Taxation has existed for thousands of years in various forms, dating back to ancient kingdoms (Sumer, 4,000 BC; Egypt, 3,000 BC). Over time, it has evolved and adapted to new economic and social realities. Yet the international component of taxation is fairly recent, dating back to the mid-19th century, when the notion of permanent establishment first appeared in European mercantile laws and case law governing subnational-level disputes involving business activities conducted across regions by enterprises not registered therein. Prussia first used the term "Betriebsstätte" in 1845 in its Industrial Code and later in 1885 in its internal tax law. Later, the term was incorporated into the first ever tax treaty concluded in 1899 between the Austro-Hungarian Empire and Prussia. By 1909, the German Double Taxation Act contained a definition of permanent establishment (box 1.1).

After the First World War, the notion of permanent establishment became widely used in tax treaties (box 1.2). However, efforts by the League of Nations to develop a universally accepted definition failed, and important discrepancies existed across countries regarding the tax treatment of several related aspects. Indeed, countries' positions evolved over time, and countries often would conclude tax treaties containing definitions of permanent establishment contrary to those in their own internal tax laws. Unfortunately, only moderate progress has been made toward advancing, unifying, and defining the notion of permanent establishment. Instead, the partisan interests and normative profusion of international organizations and countries have resulted in endless versions of the notion, increasing the complexity of the issue.

Box 1.1 Background on the Relevance of the Permanent Establishment Notion

It is common for jurisdictions to treat residents and nonresidents differently for tax purposes. As a general rule, nonresidents are liable for tax on income derived in a jurisdiction. While the individuals or companies deriving the income are not resident in the jurisdiction, they have clearly benefited from the infrastructure, market, and other features of the jurisdiction and should contribute to the jurisdiction by way of tax on profits derived in it. Resident taxpayers are commonly taxed on their income from all sources, although some jurisdictions assess residents in the same way as nonresidents, imposing tax only on income sourced in the jurisdiction. Another small group of jurisdictions impose tax on residents on a remittance basis, with income, including amounts derived abroad, considered taxable only when the funds are transferred to the jurisdiction in which the taxpayer resides.

The risk of double taxation coincided with the spread of income tax after the First World War. If source countries levy tax on nonresidents deriving income from them and resident countries impose tax on the worldwide income of residents, income derived from sources abroad could be subject to tax in two jurisdictions: the source country and the residence country. Initially, residence jurisdictions sought to relieve the double taxation through unilateral actions. Three methods were used: (a) a credit for tax paid abroad on foreign-source income, (b) an exemption for income from abroad that had been subject to tax in the source country, and (c) a deduction for foreign tax, providing partial relief only. A feature of the unilateral solution to double taxation was that the source country ended up with first and primary taxing rights, leaving the residence country with some residual rights only.

Accordingly, the early adoption of the concept of permanent establishment in international tax treaties, well before it could be defined and developed properly at a national level, prevented reaching international consensus on a universal and unique definition. The root cause that has prevented the formulation of a unique definition over the last century lies in initially adopting the wrong approach, which was to describe rather than define the notion of permanent establishment. Likewise, the current debate over taxation of the digital economy focuses more on creating new sources of taxing rights over specific digital activities and industries than on defining the traits and tax-disruptive aspects of digital business models that pose challenges to traditional tax theory and practice.[1]

Another obstacle was the conflict of national interests between countries influencing the process of creating the norm and those affected by application of the norm. The traditional notion and definitions of permanent establishment were influenced directly by the historical, geopolitical, and economic environment of the countries that participated in its design in the early 20th century. The current economic and geopolitical scenario is radically different, but the actors controlling the law-making process

Box 1.2 Evolution of the Concept of Permanent Establishment in Tax Treaties

At an early stage in the spread of income taxes, countries looked for an alternative to unilateral relief for double taxation and settled on bilateral tax treaties that divided taxing rights over income derived by nonresidents between the source country and the residence country. These early treaties incorporated the existing notion of permanent establishment as a fixed place of business for a nonresident in the source jurisdiction. In treaties that adopted this notion, the source country would agree not to tax the business profits of a nonresident unless the nonresident operated through a permanent establishment in the jurisdiction.

Following the First World War, a model treaty was developed by the League of Nations, with alternative models developed in the latter half of the 20th century by the Organisation for Economic Co-operation and Development, the United Nations, and some other organizations and individual states. Common to all of these models was the adoption of the permanent establishment rule, with source countries agreeing to forgo taxing rights over income derived by nonresidents unless the nonresidents operated through a permanent establishment in the source jurisdiction. Treaties provided some exceptions to the rule, allowing source jurisdictions to retain taxing rights, sometimes limited to capped levels, over particular types of income—most notably dividends, royalties, interest, and some capital gains—derived by nonresidents even when they had no permanent establishment in the jurisdiction.

Giving up all taxing rights over business profits, subject to the exceptions noted, may appear to be a rule substantially lopsided in favor of capital-exporting residence countries. The concern may be exaggerated for two reasons, however. The first reason is that the source country's claim to have taxing rights over business profits other than specified types of investment income derived by a nonresident is difficult to establish if the nonresident has no continuing presence in the source jurisdiction. The second reason is a pragmatic matter. While it is not difficult to use withholding taxes to impose tax on interest, dividends, royalties, and, to a lesser extent, capital gains derived by a nonresident, there are practical difficulties in collecting tax on active business profits where the taxpayer does not have a continuing presence in the jurisdiction.

The development of the digital economy has upended the traditional approach by making it possible for firms to offer a wide range of services in a jurisdiction and to derive income from the provision of those services without having a presence in the jurisdiction at all. The ease of communication via the internet, combined with the ability to attribute significant values to intangible assets and rights, opened the door for multinational enterprises to minimize their taxes by shifting profits out of host countries by means of transfer pricing: subsidiaries or permanent establishments in higher-tax jurisdictions could "buy" services or rights from related enterprises in the same multinational group located in low-tax jurisdictions.

are the same. The 1932–33 League of Nations' *Report on Taxation of Foreign and National Enterprises* states, "The major number of questions are presented by industrial enterprises in the United States of America, the United Kingdom, Germany and other European countries, and Japan, which manufacture in those countries and sell in the territory of other countries throughout the world" (Carroll 1932, 1933). Therefore, to protect their business activities abroad, they limited the notion of permanent establishment and narrowed its scope by imposing increasing limitations and exclusions. In this context, the rich countries defined the 20th-century modern notion of permanent establishment similarly to what is happening with current efforts to address the tax challenges of the digital economy.

However, today's new paradigm has reversed traditional roles: low- and middle-income countries manufacture tangible goods and sell them in the territories of high-income countries, while high-income countries export digital content and services remotely worldwide through digital means, creating the so-called digital economy. Accordingly, high-income countries are broadening the traditional notion of permanent establishment (Base Erosion and Profit Shifting [BEPS] Action 7), while, at the same time, opposing initiatives to introduce a new significant economic presence test that might help to capture the new digital business activity that takes place in a territory without any physical presence. Building on John Rawls's theory of "justice as fairness" (Rawls 1971), any universal definition of a given notion should neither take into account specific countries' interests nor factor in historical, geopolitical, or economic motives. Instead, it should be guided solely by technical considerations. Only in this way will the definition be able to stand the test of time and adapt easily to new realities, irrespective of the means used or the circumstances surrounding the performance of a business activity in a specific territory. This definition applies not only to the notion of permanent establishment, but also to the tax treatment of the digital economy, which should be determined based on the defining traits of the digital business activity.

In this context, we have conducted a comprehensive tax analysis of the digital economy and have sought to develop an appropriate tax response that aligns with traditional tax theory and helps to bridge tax principles, tax policy, and tax administration with the digital economy. Our work aims to learn from lessons from the past.

G-20 Mandate on Taxing the Digital Economy

Back in the 19th century, the tax-disruptive reality that prompted the appearance of the notion of permanent establishment was the physical presence in a foreign territory to conduct a business activity, either manufacturing or selling, therein. Nowadays, in the 21st century, the digital economy has soared as a result of the spread of broadband internet access that, combined with the advent of advanced mobile networks and mass access to digital devices, has facilitated the online distribution of digital content to a borderless market of worldwide users, without the need for a physical presence.

In 1998, at the Ottawa Ministerial Conference entitled "A Borderless World: Realizing the Potential of Electronic Commerce," the Taxation Framework Conditions published by the Organisation for Economic Co-operation and Development (OECD) were endorsed by member countries and nonmember economies as well as by the business community (OECD 1998). On the one hand, this document provided the principles that should guide governments in their approach to the taxation of e-commerce, stating that e-commerce should be treated in a similar way to traditional commerce and emphasizing the need to avoid any discriminatory treatment, in compliance with the neutrality principle. On the other hand, that same year, the World Trade Organization approved a ban on tariffs for digital trade, which has been renewed ever since and is still in effect.

By 2001, the OECD had narrowed the focus in the area of direct taxation to key issues like the application of tax treaty concepts to e-commerce and the allocation of income to a permanent establishment involved in e-commerce transactions (OECD 2001). However, given the absolute lack of physical presence of digital business models and the limitations of the notion of traditional permanent establishment as a nexus rule, tax systems proved unable to capture the digital economy under existing tax norms. Better results were achieved in the area of indirect taxation,[2] where much policy work was advanced in how consumption taxes should be applied to e-commerce. Unfortunately, the direct taxation of e-commerce remained a pending issue to be addressed later.

In 2013, the OECD addressed the impact of digitalization on international taxation through the Base Erosion and Profit Shifting (BEPS) Action Plan (OECD 2013).[3] Since then, interest in and relevance of the topic have continued to grow. In 2015, OECD published *Addressing the Tax Challenges of the Digital Economy*, which recognized the existence of a new value creation paradigm and the emergence of new digital business models (OECD 2015). In 2017, the lack of a regulatory framework for the rapidly digitalizing economy and the legal uncertainty that it generated for taxpayers and governments led the G-20 Finance Ministers to ask the OECD to deliver an interim report by 2018 on the implications of digitalization for taxation. Following the report's publication (OECD 2018), the G-20 mandated the need to reach a consensus-based solution on addressing the (direct) tax challenges of the digitalization of the economy by 2020. The G-20 entrusted the OECD's Inclusive Framework on BEPS with this mandate, and the Steering Group, supported by the OECD Secretariat, has been working extensively on it.

In the meantime, some countries have adopted unilateral measures to tax the digital economy. In 2016, India introduced the first-ever turnover-based equalization levy on business-to-business (B2B) online advertising payments made to nonresident digital service suppliers. Following the failed attempt of the European Union (EU) to introduce an EU-wide turnover-based digital services tax (DST), several countries (Austria, the Czech Republic, France, India, Italy, Spain, Turkey, the United Kingdom) have enacted their own DSTs as interim measures until the G-20 reaches a consensus-based solution. Some other countries (India, Italy, the Slovak Republic) and economies (Taiwan, China) are introducing a significant economic presence test and amending their definitions of permanent establishment. Finally, one country (Turkey) has also imposed a withholding tax on e-payments.

It is important to recognize that there are significant theoretical and practical differences in the range of unilateral measures adopted as well as in the OECD's Unified Approach proposals (box 1.3).

Box 1.3 Summary of Direct Tax Measures That Target the Digital Economy

OECD/Inclusive Framework Pillar One proposal

The Pillar One proposal outlines new profit allocation rules for certain consumer-facing businesses. The profit is allocated using simplified, formulaic principles, including a fixed baseline return for distribution and marketing functions as well a share of the group's overall residual profits. Where there is no existing taxing right, the proposal prescribes rules for establishing a new taking right ("nexus") in market jurisdictions, which can apply irrespective of physical presence. If such a nexus were triggered, the profits would be calculated based on a share of the group's overall residual profits.

Withholding on digital services

These measures create and/or implement (by acting as a collection mechanism) a source taxing right over payments made by residents to nonresidents in respect of digital services. Withholding taxes, which are already commonplace for royalty, interest, and dividend payments, can be especially effective for taxing nonresidents with no physical presence in a jurisdiction, although the practicalities of withholding an amount in respect to tax and then remitting it to the tax administration mean that this mechanism is better suited to payments made by businesses than by consumers.

Digital permanent establishments

These measures give jurisdictions the right to tax nonresident businesses that have a sustained economic interaction with their economies. This approach can apply even if the business has no physical presence in that jurisdiction. A taxable presence is deemed if, for example, the business has a sufficient level of sales or user engagement in the jurisdiction.

There are considerable uncertainties about how profit is to be allocated to the "nexus" and, in cases where a permanent establishment is deemed, how existing attribution principles apply.

Digital services tax (DST)

These measures seek to directly tax businesses earning income from certain digital services, such as online advertising and intermediary services. Some DSTs seek to tax the income earned by digital service providers by reference to fees paid either directly or indirectly by users or residents in their jurisdiction. Other DSTs apportion global digital services revenue indirectly based on the number of users, views (advertising services), or transactions (intermediary services) in the jurisdiction.

Equalization levy

This measure, introduced by India, imposes tax on certain activities of e-commerce operators. Previously the levy only applied to advertising; however, in 2020 the levy was expanded to cover the sale of goods, provision of services, and/or the facilitation thereof (for example, through a platform) by an e-commerce operator.

The vast majority of countries worldwide have not adopted unilateral digital direct taxes, although some are currently analyzing their benefits and disadvantages as interim measures. The first G-20 Finance and Central Bank Deputies Meeting in 2019 reflected the lack of consensus on the use of interim measures; while some countries (Canada, United States) oppose them because they may give rise to adverse consequences, other countries (France, the United Kingdom) argue that the challenges do not outweigh the need to ensure that tax is paid on digital services supplied in market jurisdictions. If countries do not reach a consensus, unilateral measures could proliferate, fragmenting the international tax scenario and resulting in double taxation.

The G-20 mandate refers to the tax challenges posed by the digital economy in the area of direct taxation. It covers not only cross-border transactions, but also domestic ones, which are harder for tax authorities to monitor given the intangible nature of digital content. Accordingly, tax administration challenges affect not only market jurisdictions, but also residence jurisdictions. Therefore, reaching a consensus-based global solution requires multilateral cooperation rather than uncoordinated unilateral actions. Although two-thirds of the countries worldwide have signed onto the Inclusive Framework on BEPS, if the solution is to be coordinated and implemented globally, the remaining countries must also join the debate and have their voices heard. Such participation is needed to ensure the buy-in of the entire international community, using whichever channels are needed.

Market Jurisdictions' Tax Claims: On What Basis?

Market jurisdictions have spotted an opportunity to expand their tax sovereignty and to claim new taxing rights over the digital economy. In the absence of any physical presence of the digital supplier in the market jurisdiction, this expansion clearly contravenes the tenets of traditional tax theory, which allocates taxing rights to residence countries. On the quest for justifications to support these tax claims, some proposals have resorted to new paradigms of value creation and innovative tax nexus and profit allocation methods (box 1.4)—for example, the presumptive value created by the interaction between different user groups, which encompasses positive externalities that are captured and monetized by multisided digital platforms. In short, the current debate revolves around the question of whether the countries where users are located are entitled to tax the value that users contribute to digital businesses that are tax-resident abroad. Such tax claims are intimately linked to both the notion of permanent establishment (taxable presence) and the notion of source taxation (taxable source).

It is of utmost importance to clarify the basis on which market jurisdictions claim taxing rights over foreign digital suppliers operating in their territory without any physical presence. Several options are available for new nexus rules:

- *Tax claims on the basis of taxable presence*, by way of formulating a revised notion of permanent establishment that overcomes the physical presence limitation of new

---

Box 1.4 Is There a Need for a New Paradigm of Value Creation?

The combined pressures of transfer pricing and the limited application of existing tax norms to international digital economy enterprises led the Organisation for Economic Co-operation and Development and nonmember countries that joined the Base Erosion and Profit Shifting (BEPS) program to propose allocating the profits derived by multinational enterprises, including those providing digital supplies and services, between countries on the basis of where "value is created." There was, however, no agreement on what constitutes value creation, and the concept remained vague and undefined. Traditionally, jurisdictions looking for indicators of value creation when seeking to allocate a share of profits by a multinational or multistate enterprise focused on three inputs to value creation:

- The value of tangible capital employed in the jurisdiction (premises and equipment) relative to the total tangible capital of the firm
- The cost of labor in the jurisdiction compared to total labor costs
- The value of sales in the jurisdiction.

The question that tax policy makers are facing now is whether these inputs, adopted in the era of traditional commerce, are fair indicators for determining the share of global profits with a source in each contributing jurisdiction.

---

digital business models that operate either remotely or with a limited local presence and derive income from a market jurisdiction (significant economic presence)

- *Tax claims on the basis of taxable source*, by way of establishing a new source of taxable income deemed to arise from value creation within a market jurisdiction (user participation, marketing intangibles)
- *Other measures that counteract the use of tax avoidance schemes*, although their scope is much wider than just digital economy (diverted profits tax).

Unfortunately, as a result of the urge to secure new sources of tax revenue, some countries have rushed to pass unilateral tax measures (digital services taxes, withholding taxes, expanded permanent establishment rules) that aim to capture some parts of the digital economy without previously conducting a thorough analysis of whether such measures conform to tax theory principles.[4] Such improvisation creates juridical double taxation for foreign digital suppliers, which are taxed on their income in their residence country as well as taxed on their revenue in the market jurisdictions where they operate. Such double taxation jeopardizes their financial viability.

From an economic double taxation perspective, policy makers have overlooked the most basic economic implications of unilaterally introducing revenue taxes on foreign digital suppliers without a physical presence in the market jurisdiction, since not only is the same transaction taxed from both the supplier side (direct taxation) and the customer side (indirect taxation), but it is taxed thrice in case certain functions of the digital value chain are outsourced to local providers (storage, distribution, customer care), which are subject to tax as residents in the market jurisdiction. Indeed, by imposing new revenue-based taxes on foreign digital suppliers, while also taxing local entities that provide logistical support for the operations of those foreign digital suppliers, the market jurisdiction is double dipping[5] on the same transaction from the viewpoint of direct taxation.

Market countries that claim taxing rights are resorting to two different strategies with the aim of minimizing conflict with existing national taxation systems, while still creating double taxation. First, in the absence of an applicable tax treaty between the residence and the market jurisdictions, some countries have expanded the scope of the domestic definition of nexus rule beyond the traditional notion, allowing them to capture income that foreign digital suppliers derive from within the territory. For example, in 2015, Saudi Arabia used administrative guidelines to introduce the concept of virtual service permanent establishment, which did not consider the physical presence of nonresident service providers for establishing the nexus to the source country. Along the same lines, countries like India and Italy have amended their definitions of permanent establishment to introduce a significant economic presence test. Second, some countries have enacted new revenue-based taxes that avoid falling within the scope of income tax treaties, since the tax base is turnover rather than income. This is the case of India's equalization levy and European digital services taxes, all of which raise the issue of potentially taxing nonexistent profit for companies with either very tight profit margins or unused tax losses.

In the absence of an international tax system and a global authority, the digital debate comes down to a clash of national economic interests, where market jurisdictions claim new taxing rights at the expense of eroding the tax bases of residence countries. Since traditional tax theory supports the status quo, the only way that market jurisdictions have to claim new sources of tax revenue is to dismantle traditional tax principles. Moreover, unless countries are willing to renegotiate the allocation of taxing rights, which is unlikely, the ultimate losers will be customers, who will bear the additional tax burden arising from double taxation.

Back to Basics: Philosophy of the Report

This report aims to analyze and understand tax-disruptive aspects of new digital business models as a first step to ascertaining the need for new measures to address the tax challenges of the digitalization of the economy. Unlike many proposals, our work focuses strictly on the tax aspects of the digital economy; it does not use the digital economy as a pretext for dismantling the existing international tax framework or for altering the current tax sovereignty status quo. The G-20 mandate is simple and clear. Therefore, policy makers should refrain from distorting the scope of the work and regulating beyond it, as is unfortunately happening with some initiatives that unduly extend their policy work to business models that bear no connection with the digital economy (consumer-facing businesses under OECD's Secretariat Proposal for a Unified Approach). Although some aspects of the digital economy may exacerbate the risk of base erosion, this situation should not be used as a pretext for passing new tax norms that address tax issues not related to the digital economy (shifting profit to entities subject to no or very low taxation under Pillar Two of the OECD's Programme of Work), which clearly fall outside the scope of the G-20 mandate (box 1.5).

Box 1.5 The OECD's Programme of Work: Pillars One and Two

The Organisation for Economic Co-operation and Development's Programme of Work is a document that explores all relevant issues and options in connection with the two pillars (OECD 2019j). Pillar One focuses on the technical options for revising the nexus and profit allocation rules (OECD 2019h). The revision of nexus rules can be addressed either from a taxable-presence perspective—that is, the connection between a taxing jurisdiction and a person deemed to be resident of it (residence-based taxation)—or from a taxable-source approach—that is, the connection between a taxing jurisdiction and income derived from within it (source-based taxation). In both cases, the nexus rules set the minimum requirements for the taxing jurisdiction to impose tax on the taxpayer. However, profit allocation rules determine which and how much profit and losses to attribute for tax purposes in relation to new taxing rights. Specifically, profit allocation rules comprise the scope of profit subject to the new taxing right (all profit or only residual profit, profit from the multinational group or only from one or some entities), the choice of method for calculating and allocating profit subject to the new taxing right (modified residual profit split method, fractional apportionment method, modified deemed profit method), and the preferred treatment of losses (symmetric or asymmetric treatment of losses, use of a claw-back mechanism).

Pillar Two addresses the continuous risk of profit shifting to entities subject to no or very low taxation (OECD 2019i). Also known as the Global Base Erosion (GloBE) proposal, Pillar Two consists of a series of coordinated rules (income inclusion rule, switch-over rule, undertaxed payments rule, subject-to-tax rule) that seek to guarantee a global minimum tax rate. To achieve this result, the rules assign new taxing rights to jurisdictions over income taxed in another jurisdiction at an effective rate below a minimum rate. Some of these rules require amendments to tax treaties (switch-over rules, subject-to-tax rule), while other rules apply only to related parties (undertaxed payments rule). This proposal aims to eliminate the exemption method from tax treaties and to replace it with the credit method, to prevent double non-taxation or taxation below the minimum rate (switch-over rule). Finally, these rules may operate alongside or even replace controlled foreign corporation (CFC) rules. Some countries have already amended their domestic tax laws based on Pillar Two discussions.

It is essential to go back to basics—that is, to validate all proposals in light of traditional tax theory on which worldwide tax systems and international tax norms like tax treaties are based—with special emphasis on compliance with traditional tax principles. Failure to do so will result in tax measures disconnected from countries' own tax systems. Moreover, it is necessary to discard all assumptions and to revisit the most basic tax notions that inform the design of sound tax policy and tax administration practices. Current initiatives have ignored this validation process and have jumped directly into creating new taxing rights (Amount A under OECD's Unified Approach consisting of a share of deemed residual profit allocated to market jurisdictions using a formulaic approach), without having a valid technical rationale to support the change. Needless to say, the G-20 mandate does not give policy makers carte blanche to disregard the foundations of our tax systems and to get creative in ways that do not conform to tax theory principles. Besides, any solution should be the result of a technical analysis of the tax challenges posed by the digital economy. Accordingly, the starting point should be to assess the scope of the digital economy and its distinctive features and elements that may justify the need for new tax rules and then to determine whether solving such tax challenges requires a tax policy response, new tax administration mechanisms, both, or none. Sometimes, doing nothing is doing something, as long as it is properly justified.

Organization of the Report

The report is organized into seven chapters, including this one, that are intended to provide a comprehensive analysis of the tax-disruptive aspects of new digital business models. Chapter 2 examines the challenges of taxing the digital economy, including the scope and features that distinguish the digital economy from the traditional economy, which may require a revision of the current tax rules. With this aim, we have developed an inclusive typology of the digital elements of economic transactions, a categorization of transactions and business models, and a complete taxonomy of tax-disruptive digital business models, all of which are analyzed against traditional business models in order to identify the challenges of taxing the digital economy.

Chapter 3 analyzes those tax principles that have traditionally informed and guided the development of tax systems and have a direct impact on taxing the digital economy: horizontal equity, benefit principle, neutrality principle, tax sovereignty, and administrative feasibility. We have determined the scope of digital and tax-disruptive digital business models that are taxable in market jurisdictions as well as the interplay of such tax principles as applied to the digital economy.

Chapter 4 analyzes the economic and legal consequences of taxing the digital economy, such as the double taxation of digital suppliers, revenue recognition issues arising from the need to monetize value, the tax impact of legal structures, monetization strategies used by digital business models, and the double revenue threshold mechanism.

Chapter 5 analyzes the impact of the digital economy on the taxing rights of countries as well as the new nexus rule based on sales proposed by the OECD's Unified Approach. It also examines the distinction between routine and residual profits and revised profit allocation rules, compares the use of presumptive taxation (turnover tax) by digital services taxes to income taxation, and considers taxation of other types of digital income.

Chapter 6 analyzes tax administration issues related to taxing the digital economy, such as the tax registration of foreign digital companies; assessment, accrual, and application of presumptive digital taxes; and collection and enforcement of digital tax claims.

Chapter 7 proposes the creation of a new digital data tax (DDT) and a global internet tax agency (GITA), which would be entrusted with supporting all countries in administering the digital data tax. It analyzes all defining elements of this original proposal, which would overcome the challenges posed by current tax measures and initiatives, while abiding by traditional tax theory.

A final chapter presents the main conclusions from the analysis of the tax-disruptive aspects of digital business models and provides a critical assessment on the future of taxation of the internet.

Notes

1. Some scholars have raised concerns, shared by us, about the misuse of the digital debate to increase the taxing rights of source countries. Digital taxes would be only the first step toward the greater goal of reforming the current scope of source taxing rights.

2. The reason why better results have been achieved in the area of indirect taxation may be because businesses that can pass on indirect taxes are less concerned about them, so long as they get their input refunds.

3. The BEPS Action Plan consists of 15 actions intended to equip governments with domestic and international rules and instruments to address tax avoidance, ensuring that profits are taxed where economic activities generating the profits are performed and where value is created. For a complete and detailed explanation, refer to the BEPS section of the OECD official website.

4. Some international tax experts argue that there may be a solid policy grounding for implementing such unilateral tax measures on the basis of overlapping policy objectives with existing practices (source taxation of service income) and with existing norms (Article 12A of the United Nations Model Convention on Fees for Technical Services). The United Nations is currently discussing a new article to its Model Convention (Article 12B), which explicitly provides a source taxation right over digitally provided services. This new approach would make it possible to reconcile digital services taxes and withholding taxes with the principles of traditional tax theory. This perspective has been considered internally at the World Bank, and a discussion is likely to be published in a forthcoming discussion paper by Ben Stewart and Colin Clavey (Stewart and Clavey 2021).

5. Some scholars have argued that double dipping is not relevant in economic terms. Instead, they consider that what really matters is the total effective tax rate, not who gets it. They are absolutely right from an economic viewpoint. However, from a legal perspective, it is extremely relevant to establish the rationale behind taxing rights, their allocation, and those who are subject to them. A low effective tax rate cannot serve as a pretext for recognizing or creating new taxing rights without proper legal justification. Indeed, as more taxing rights are recognized over the same economic transaction, the greater is the risk that those entitled to such taxing rights will alter the combined total effective tax rate. Double dipping also may have administrative and compliance costs implications.

Bibliography

Adams, Charles. 2001. *For Good and Evil: The Impact of Taxes on the Course of Civilization*. 2nd ed. Lanham, MD: Madison Books.

Bunn, Daniel, Elke Asen, and Cristina Enache. 2020. *Digital Taxation around the World*. Washington, DC: Tax Foundation.

Carroll, Mitchell. 1932. *Report on Taxation of Foreign and National Enterprises: A Study of the Tax Systems and the Methods of Allocation of the Profits of Enterprises Operating in More Than One Country*. Vol. 1. Geneva: League of Nations.

Carroll, Mitchell. 1933. *Report on Taxation of Foreign and National Enterprises: A Study of the Tax Systems and the Methods of Allocation of the Profits of Enterprises Operating in More Than One Country*. Vols. 2 and 3. Geneva: League of Nations.

Faulhaber, Lilian. 2019. "Taxing Tech: The Future of Digital Taxation." *Virginia Tax Review* 39 (2): 145–96.

Förster, Hartmut, Stefan Greil, and Arnim Hilse. 2020. "Taxing the Digital Economy: The OECD Secretariat's New Transfer Pricing A-B-C and Alternative Courses of Action." *International Transfer Pricing Journal* 27 (1).

Krever, Richard, and Kerrie Sadiq. 2019. "Actions to Counter Base Erosion and Profit Shifting: A General Report." In *Tax Design and Administration in a Post-BEPS Era: A Study of Key Reform Measures in 18 Jurisdictions*, edited by Kerrie Sadiq, Adrian Sawyer, and Bronwyn McCredie, 1–24. Birmingham: Fiscal Publications.

OECD (Organisation for Economic Co-operation and Development). 1998. "Electronic Commerce: Taxation Framework Conditions." Report by the Committee on Fiscal Affairs, as presented at OECD Ministerial Conference "A Borderless World: Realising the Potential of Electronic Commerce," OECD, Ottawa, October 8, 1998.

OECD (Organisation for Economic Co-operation and Development). 2001. "Taxation and Electronic Commerce. Implementing the Ottawa Taxation Framework Conditions." OECD, Paris.

OECD (Organisation for Economic Co-operation and Development). 2013. *Action Plan on Base Erosion and Profit Shifting*. Paris: OECD Publishing.

OECD (Organisation for Economic Co-operation and Development). 2015. *Addressing the Tax Challenges of the Digital Economy, Action 1— 2015 Final Report*. OECD/G-20 Base Erosion and Profit Shifting Project. Paris: OECD.

OECD (Organisation for Economic Co-operation and Development). 2017a. "International VAT/GST Guidelines." OECD, Paris, April 12, 2017.

OECD (Organisation for Economic Co-operation and Development). 2017b. "Mechanisms for the Effective Collection of VAT/GST Where the Supplier Is Not Located in the Jurisdiction of Taxation." OECD, Paris.

OECD (Organisation for Economic Co-operation and Development). 2018. *Tax Challenges Arising from Digitalization—Interim Report 2018: Inclusive Framework on BEPS*. Paris: OECD.

OECD (Organisation for Economic Co-operation and Development). 2019a. "Addressing the Tax Challenges of the Digitalisation of the Economy." Policy note approved by the Inclusive Framework on BEPS, OECD, Paris, January 23, 2019.

OECD (Organisation for Economic Co-operation and Development). 2019b. "Addressing the Tax Challenges of the Digitalisation of the Economy." Public consultation document, OECD Secretariat, Paris, February 13–March 6, 2019.

OECD (Organisation for Economic Co-operation and Development). 2019c. "Background Note on the Programme of Work, Steering Group of the Inclusive Framework on BEPS, 24 April 2019." OECD, Paris.

OECD (Organisation for Economic Co-operation and Development). 2019d. "Compilation of Comments from the Steering Group on Pillar 1 & 2." Steering Group of the Inclusive Framework, OECD, Paris, April 8, 2019.

OECD (Organisation for Economic Co-operation and Development). 2019e. "Compilation of Comments on the Table on the Programme of Work." Comments received for the Inclusive Framework Meeting, OECD, Paris, May 28–29 2019.

OECD (Organisation for Economic Co-operation and Development). 2019f. "Draft Summary Record: Meeting of the Steering Group of the Inclusive Framework on BEPS, 8–9 April 2019, as Approved by the Steering Group on 29 April 2019." OECD, Paris.

OECD (Organisation for Economic Co-operation and Development). 2019g. "Fractional Apportionment Method in the Context of Addressing the Tax Challenges of the Digitalisation of the Economy." Technical note prepared by the OECD Secretariat, Paris, June 17, 2019.

OECD (Organisation for Economic Co-operation and Development). 2019h. "Issue Note on Pillar 1—Develop a Consensus Solution to the Direct Tax Challenges Arising from the Digitalization of the Economy." Steering Group of Inclusive Framework on BEPS, OECD, Paris, March 25, 2019.

OECD (Organisation for Economic Co-operation and Development). 2019i. "Issue Note on Pillar 2—GloBE Proposal." Note to the Steering Group of the Inclusive Framework, OECD, Paris, March 25, 2019.

OECD (Organisation for Economic Co-operation and Development). 2019j. "Programme of Work to Develop a Consensus Solution to the Tax Challenges Arising from the Digitalisation of the Economy, as Approved by the Inclusive Framework on BEPS on 28 May 2019." OECD, Paris.

OECD (Organisation for Economic Co-operation and Development). 2019k. "Residual Profit Split Methods in the Context of Addressing the Tax Challenges of the Digitalisation of the Economy." Technical note, OECD Secretariat, Paris, June 18, 2019.

OECD (Organisation for Economic Co-operation and Development). 2019l. "The Role of Digital Platforms in the Collection of VAT/GST on Online Sales." OECD, Paris, March.

OECD (Organisation for Economic Co-operation and Development). 2019m. "Secretariat Proposal for a 'Unified Approach' under Pillar One." Public consultation document, OECD Secretariat, Paris, October 9–November 12, 2019.

OECD (Organisation for Economic Co-operation and Development). 2020a. "Model Rules for Reporting by Platform Operators with Respect to Sellers in the Sharing and Gig Economy." OECD Secretariat, Paris, July 3, 2020.

OECD (Organisation for Economic Co-operation and Development). 2020b. "OECD Secretary-General Tax Report to G-20 Finance Ministers and Central Bank Governors, Riyadh, Saudi Arabia, February 2020." OECD, Paris.

OECD (Organisation for Economic Co-operation and Development). 2020c. "Public Consultation Document, Reports on the Pillar One and Pillar Two Blueprints, 12 October 2020–14 December 2020: OECD/G-20 Inclusive Framework on BEPS," OECD Publishing, Paris.

OECD (Organisation for Economic Co-operation and Development). 2020d. "Statement by the OECD/G-20 Inclusive Framework on BEPS on the Two-Pillar Approach to Address the Tax Challenges Arising from the Digitalisation of the Economy, as Approved by the OECD/G-20 Inclusive Framework on BEPS on 29–30 January 2020." OECD, Paris.

OECD (Organisation for Economic Co-operation and Development). 2020e. "Tax Challenges Arising from Digitalisation—Report on Pillar One Blueprint: Inclusive Framework on BEPS." OECD/G-20 Base Erosion and Profit Shifting Project, OECD Publishing, Paris.

OECD (Organisation for Economic Co-operation and Development). 2020f. "Tax Challenges Arising from Digitalisation—Report on Pillar Two Blueprint: Inclusive Framework on BEPS." OECD/G-20 Base Erosion and Profit Shifting Project, OECD Publishing, Paris.

Office of the United States Trade Representative. 2019. "Report on France's Digital Services Tax Prepared in the Investigation under Section 301 of the Trade Act of 1974, Issued on 2 December 2019." Office of the US Trade Representative, Washington, DC.

Rawls, John. 1971. *Justice as Fairness*. Cambridge, MA: Belknap Press.

Schreiber, Ulrich. 2020. "Remarks on the OECD/G-20 Program of Work: Profit Allocation and Minimum Taxation." Working paper, Mannheim University.

Stewart, Ben, and Colin Clavey. 2021 (forthcoming). "Digital Services Tax: Country Practice and Technical Challenges." MTI Discussion Paper, Macroeconomics, Trade, and Investment Global Practice, World Bank, Washington, DC.

CHAPTER 2

Tax Challenges of Taxing the Digital Economy

To define the digital economy, it is essential to understand the elements of an economic transaction that may involve the use of digital technology. Some of those digital elements may pose challenges to the application of traditional tax rules that may require special tax measures. Based on the presence or not of such tax-disruptive digital elements, digital transactions and digital business models are subcategorized for tax purposes into tax disruptive or not. The tax analysis focuses mainly on the subcategory of tax-disruptive digital business models, comparing them to traditional business models and other tax challenges.

Digital Elements of Economic Transactions

The first challenge is to understand what digital means. Digital refers to binary-digit data-encoding technology. A binary code represents text, computer processor instructions, or other data using a two-symbol system of zeros and ones. Something is said to be digital if it uses such data-encoding technology, which enables the transfer of data worldwide in practically real time at zero marginal cost.

Any element of an economic transaction that relies on this data-encoding technology is considered a digital element. Likewise, any economic transaction and, by extension, any business model that comprises one or more digital elements (digital communication, digital content, digital automation, digital distribution, digital payment) is categorized as digital for taxonomical purposes and is considered part of the digital economy. For tax purposes, special emphasis is placed on the analysis and impact of economic transactions and digital business models that have digital elements with tax-disruptive aspects. These transactions and models form a separate subcategory of tax-disruptive digital business models, which are the main focus of our analysis in this report. Therefore, tax-disruptive digital elements, such as digital content, digital distribution, and digital automation, are only present in tax-disruptive digital business models, since they are interconnected and operate together. For example, digital content can only be delivered online through digital distribution, and supply of and access to digital content are mostly digitally auto-mated. Moreover, digital distribution uses the internet as a delivery channel, which also operates as an element of digital communication. Table 2.1 contains a typology of the digital elements of economic transactions.

Tax-Disruptive Aspects of Digital Elements

Some digital elements may disrupt the way transactions have been traditionally carried out, monitored, and taxed. This section analyzes which digital elements have tax-disruptive features that may require special tax treatment and how the presence of such elements affects the categorization of business models. Digital business models that contain tax-disruptive digital elements are grouped into a subcategory of tax-disruptive digital business models. They are the main focus of our analysis, given the challenges they pose for taxing the digital economy.

Table 2.1 Typology of the Digital Elements of Transactions

Digital elements	Description	Examples
Digital communication	Networking infrastructure used by the parties to an economic transaction to connect and communicate with each other	Internet (e-mail, internet telephony, online streaming)
Digital content (tax-disruptive)	Any content that exists in the form of digital data or digital object; digital content relies heavily on intangibles since its support is digital (bits) instead of physical (atoms) and is intrinsically linked to the existence of digital technology	E-books, software, domain names, mobile apps, social media, digital audio, digital images, websites, World Wide Web (www), digital video streaming, website hosting, webpages, cybersecurity, website positioning, antivirus protection, cloud data storage, search engine, internet access, online games, cloud-based apps, digital data and databases, digital platforms
Digital automation (tax-disruptive)	Minimum or no human intervention is required on the provider side since the process is automated and controlled by consumers, who contribute data and content and customize the content	Search engines, data mining, media streaming, visa processing, price comparison, online booking, customer support, translation, employee analytics, résumé drafting, ticketing
Digital distribution (tax-disruptive)	Distribution over an online delivery channel, like the internet, thus bypassing physical distribution methods	E-mail, e-commerce, online gambling, online gaming, peer-to-peer file-sharing networks, online advertising, online tax filling, online digital media streaming, software and video game downloads, e-learning, digital content delivery networks
Digital payment	Payment methods based on binary encoding technology	Electronic funds transfer methods (for example, credit and debit card payments, automated teller machine transfers, wire transfers, stored-value cards, online bill payments)

Source: Original table for this publication.

Digital elements are considered tax-disruptive when they increase the complexity of traditional tax administration and tax enforcement practices. For some elements (communication, payment), digitalization has improved their functionalities (network bandwidth capacity, data transfer, data compression, identity verification, data security, customization of consumer experience). For other elements (content, distribution, automation), the spread of digital technology has enabled new economic realities that have altered the traditional business ecosystem and prompted the rise of tax-disruptive digital business models.

It is important to distinguish between the use of digital technology to enhance existing business functions (communication, money transfer) that were previously fulfilled through traditional channels (for communication, person-to-person, telephony, radio, television, postal mail, newspapers; for money transfer, money orders, traveler's checks, magnetic stripe bank and nonbank credit cards, bank checks) and the core role of digital technology in the advent of tax-disruptive realities (intangible content, online platforms, online delivery, zero marginal cost supply) that did not exist previously and may render tax norms and economic postulates inapplicable.

To begin with, the use of financial sector–based digital payment methods (electronic funds transfer systems, like credit and debit card payments, automated teller machine transfers, wire transfers, stored-value cards, online bill payments) barely disrupts traditional business and tax practices, since similar methods of transferring money have been used for decades in traditional transactions. In fact, financial sector–based money transfer payments provide tax authorities with greater control and monitoring mechanisms. Therefore, digital payment methods based on electronic funds transfer are not considered a tax-disruptive digital element.

Similarly, on its own, the communication channel has limited impact on tax enforcement, since digital communication does not differ significantly from traditional telecommunication channels like telephony, postal mail, radio, newspapers, or television. Assuming that the other elements to the economic transaction are not digital, using the internet to communicate with customers to arrange a physical transaction does not pose major tax challenges: the tangible nature of the content of the transaction and the channel of distribution allows effective control and taxation by the tax authorities. In contrast, using the internet to attract users and to influence customers raises some tax concerns because the internet functions as a digital channel for delivering online advertising content; it is not just a digital channel for communicating with customers. Therefore, using the internet as a digital communication channel is not considered as a tax-disruptive digital element.

The digital automation of business processes has enabled digital business models to reach scale without mass at zero marginal cost. The physical workforce (human workers) have been replaced by the use of digital innovation to streamline business processes and maintain a competitive edge. Digital automation intervenes in the supply of digital content (media-streaming platforms) and is only present in tax-disruptive digital business models. Moreover, it always requires the internet as a communication channel. So, digital automation is considered as a tax-disruptive digital element.

Lastly, digital content and digital distribution are analyzed jointly, since they are interdependent: only digital content can be distributed digitally, and digital content can only be distributed digitally. Both elements have drastically transformed the supply of goods and services by making it possible to do so without a physical presence in the market jurisdiction. This change poses a very serious tax challenge, since tax authorities may not even be aware that such digital transactions are taking place within their territory. For example, no customs need to be cleared, neither raw materials nor labor force intervenes, no factories or warehouses are needed, and no inventories are kept since online content is digital (bits) instead of physical (atoms). Likewise, digital distribution comprises online delivery of digital media content, either downloaded (allowing users to store it permanently) or streamed (sharing content at the user's request or on demand), which overcomes any physical barriers to trade. Therefore, both digital content and digital distribution, together with digital automation, are considered as tax-disruptive digital elements that are only present in tax-disruptive digital business models. Table 2.2 categorizes transactions and business models.

Tax-Disruptive Digital Business Models

The spread of broadband internet access not only has transformed traditional business models, but also has enabled the appearance of new digital business models, some of which pose challenges for traditional taxation. Indeed, for tax purposes, digital business models that entail tax-disruptive digital elements are categorized as tax-disruptive digital business models. Non-tax-disruptive digital business models adapt traditional business models to the digital economy by using the internet as a communication channel and by using digital technology as a tool to enhance traditional business functions. Still, the underlying goods and services are tangible and physically delivered, which allows tax authorities to be aware of the economic activity happening within their borders. The focus of our tax analysis is on tax-disruptive digital business models.

Tax-disruptive digital business models in their most basic form entail the online distribution of automated digital content (online sales, online subscription plans, online license agreements) or the granting of online access to automated digital content or multisided digital platforms that connect online users, in all cases in exchange for financial compensation (final price, subscription fee, user license fee, perpetual license fee). Therefore, tax-disruptive digital business models may adopt multiple arrangements, depending on the number of transactions and parties, the nature of the financial compensation, the type of digital content, the monetization strategy employed, the geographic scope of operations, the digital distribution technology used, and the assets and resources, functions, and risks assumed by different parties to the transactions. Another distinctive feature is the central role that users occupy in the digital value proposition. This feature must offer a valuable solution to solve an important problem or create additional benefits for the users. Consequently, users tend to influence the monetization strategies of business models.

Table 2.2 Categorization of Transactions and Business Models

Categories of transactions and their business models	Digital elements present				
	Communication	Content	Automation	Distribution	Payment
Traditional transactions and business models					
In-person transactions involving physical supply of goods and services paid using a physical payment method (babysitters, street vendors, flea markets, cash sales)	X	X	X	X	X
Digital transactions and business models					
In-person transactions involving the physical supply of goods and services paid using digital payment methods (credit card sales, online utility bill payments)	X	X	X	X	✓
Online transactions involving the physical supply of goods and services paid using a physical payment method (free posting sites for classified advertisements, like Craigslist; websites of physical retail stores to reserve goods online)	✓	X	X	X	X
Online transactions involving the physical supply of goods and services paid using a digital payment method (online marketplaces, like Amazon or eBay; online ride-hailing services, like Uber; online food delivery services, like Uber Eats; online booking of hotels, like Marriott; online stores of physical retail stores, like Zara)	✓	X	X	X	✓
Tax-disruptive digital transactions and business models					
Online transactions involving online supply of digital content, digitally automated and digitally distributed, paid using digital payment methods (online marketplaces, like Amazon; online retailers of digital content, like Apple iTunes Store or Amazon Kindle Store; digital distribution platforms, like Microsoft Store; digital media services, like Netflix or Spotify; web search engines, like Google)	✓	✓	✓	✓	✓

Source: Original table for this publication.

The following are the most common user-centered monetization strategies:

- Sale of users' demographic data (race, gender, economic status, level of education, family status, income level, employment)
- Sale of users' behavioral data (values, personality, attitudes, opinions, lifestyles, interests)
- Sale of users' activity data (browser history, purchase history, recent activity)
- Sale of user-targeted advertising (based on user traits and preferences)
- Sale of user-created content (blogs, reviews, opinions, databases, media file sharing)
- Appropriation of user-developed intangibles (video games' fan-made content, collective translations, server emulators)
- Sale of the digital business (exit) after its value has been enhanced by the contributions of users in exchange for free-of-charge access to digital content and digital platforms.

Such free-of-charge access is not really free for users, since they contribute, knowingly or not, personal data and digital content, which digital companies use as commodities and monetize. The reverse is also true: users do not contribute data and content for free; they do it in exchange for access to digital content and platforms that are supplied free of charge but have a cost for the provider. Still, users are not always aware that their personal data and user-created content are being shared, which raises concerns about data privacy that fall outside the scope of this analysis. In brief, online users act as suppliers of digital input (personal data, user-created digital content) in exchange[1] for free access to digital content and digital platforms. Afterward, digital businesses process such digital input by means of proprietary digital automation technologies (data storage, data mining, data analytics, data visualization) and extract marketable information (user-based segmentation data sets), which is monetized.

Furthermore, tax-disruptive digital business models may comprise one or multiple transactions by the same taxpayer, which aim to monetize the business idea. For this reason, at least one of the digital transactions involves financial compensation. Additional transactions may serve the purpose of obtaining digital input (user data, user-created content, user-developed intangibles, user base) that may enhance the value of the digital business (know-how, goodwill), enable the digital business model (sale of user-targeted online advertising), or be sold as a digital commodity. From a tax perspective, all costs incurred to obtain and process such digital input (free-of-charge supply of digital content, technical platform development, automation technology) should be taken into account when assessing the taxable income from the other transactions that monetize the business model (sale of digital content, subscription for online access to digital content, licensing of digital content, sale of user data and user-created digital content, sale of user-targeted online advertising services).

Table 2.3 contains a comprehensive taxonomy of tax-disruptive digital business models. Although some company examples are provided, internet companies usually develop several business activities simultaneously through different business models.

Table 2.3 Taxonomy of Tax-Disruptive Digital Business Models

Type of tax-disruptive digital business model (and examples)	Digital transactions (by the same taxpayer) to monetize a business idea and get user input
Content-related	
1. Sale of nonuser digital content (Kindle Store, Apple iTunes Store)	1.1. Online sale of digital content digitally automated and digitally distributed for a price
2. Licensing of nonuser digital content (Microsoft, IBM, Cisco, Oracle)	2.1. Online licensing to use digital content (software end user license) for a license fee
3. Subscription to nonuser digital content (Netflix, Spotify, Amazon Prime)	3.1. Online subscription to access digital content and other benefits for a subscription fee
Regulated activities	
4. Virtual banking (First Direct, ING Direct, Revolut)	4.1. Internet-only bank offering retail banking services remotely via digital channels
5. Virtual insurance (ZhongAn, Bowtie Insurance)	5.1. Internet-only insurance company offering retail insurance services via digital channels
6. Online gambling (Bet365, Bwin, Betfair, 888)	6.1. Online gambling and betting activities directly between the user and the website
Multisided platforms	
7. Online e-commerce marketplace (Amazon, Uber, Airbnb, Booking, eBay, Alibaba, Tencent, Expedia, crowdfunding platforms, online poker)	7.1. Free online access to multisided platforms 7.2. Digital platform operator acting as a broker and charging a transactional fee for each trade executed between users of the digital platform
User-related	
8. Sale of user-related data and user-contributed digital content (Facebook, Instagram, Twitter)	8.1. Online access to digital content in exchange for legal rights to sell user data and content 8.2. Sale of user-related data and digital content
9. Online user-targeted advertising (Google Ads, Amazon, LinkedIn, Alibaba, YouTube, Facebook, Reddit)	9.1. Online access to digital content in exchange for legal rights to exploit user data and content 9.2. Sale of online user-targeted advertising
10. Sale of user-related goodwill as part of the sale of a digital business (exit business strategy) (Instagram, LinkedIn, WhatsApp, Skype, Waze, YouTube, Fitbit)	10.1. Online access to digital content in exchange for legal rights to benefit from user base, user-related data, and user-created digital content 10.2. Sale of digital business (exit) whose value is enhanced by user-related goodwill

Source: Original table for this publication.

They may even use multiple business models to develop the same business activity, depending on the geographic location and the domestic tax and legal regulations.

For clarification purposes, online gambling, where users bet against the website (online casinos) must be distinguished from multisided gambling platforms, where users bet against other users and the website takes a brokerage fee (online poker). Multisided gambling platforms must be analyzed separately.

Additional explanation may be needed in relation to the telecommunication industry, which is another regulated sector, like banking, insurance, or gambling. The reason why it is not considered as a separate tax-disruptive digital business model is because internet telephony and messaging providers (WhatsApp, Skype) mostly monetize through the sale of user-related goodwill (WhatsApp was sold to Facebook; Skype was sold to Microsoft), the sale of user data and user-targeted online advertising (WhatsApp), and subscription plans for making calls or using a phone number (Skype). Therefore, internet telecommunication providers use monetization strategies that fall within other tax-disruptive digital business models, and the nature of the service provided is not unique in nature. Banking, insurance, and gambling are analyzed in chapter 3.

Moreover, unlike most providers of other digital services, internet telecommunication providers offer their digital service through the physical infrastructure of their competing traditional business models (internet service providers [ISPs], especially tier-3 ISPs that provide local access to the internet for end customers, through cable, digital subscriber line [DSL], fiber, or wireless access networks). Users need to have internet access to use internet telecommunication services (WhatsApp and Skype require an internet connection). In this special case, the tax-disruptive digital business model is dependent on its competitor, which operates as a traditional business model. Without the physical infrastructure of the traditional telecommunication business, the internet telecommunication business cannot operate; the same is true of any other internet-based business. As a consequence, the telecommunication industry is more of a backbone for the digital economy than a business model in and of itself.

Finally, to a certain extent, something similar happens with virtual banking when customers need to have access to cash. In that case, virtual banking companies are forced to enter into agreements with traditional banks that own automated teller machines so that they can connect their systems and virtual banking customers can withdraw funds. This dependence on the traditional banking system is minor compared with the central role that traditional telecommunication companies (tier-3 ISPs) play in relation to internet telecommunication providers, which fully depend on their infrastructure.

Network Effect of Multisided Digital Platforms

Many digital businesses use multisided digital platforms that create value by facilitating connections between different but interdependent user groups. Each side of the network depends on the presence of the other, as demand by one group increases demand by the other group and vice versa. This interdependence increases the value of the digital business to the extent that it attracts more users, a phenomenon known as the network effect.

This network effect is part of the user-related goodwill that enhances the value of a digital business, which is monetized when the digital business itself is sold as part of its business exit strategy. The increase in the number of users also provides a greater amount of user-related data and user-created digital content, which is either appropriated by the digital company to enhance its own business operations or sold to third parties for different purposes (to provide online user-targeted advertising services, to adapt the design of product to users' preferences, to improve service, to optimize customer support and after-sales services). Online targeted advertising is only one of the many purposes for which user-related data and user-contributed digital content may be used. Consequently, the network effect is one of the mechanisms for creating and obtaining value from digital business models based on multisided digital platforms.

One of the tax challenges associated with the network effect from multisided digital platforms is the role of data and user participation in the creation of value and how it should be taxed. In this regard, as mentioned, users supply digital input (data, digital content) in exchange for access to digital content (Google web search engine, Amazon e-commerce marketplace, Facebook social media platform, Gmail e-mail services). Basically, users trade their data and content in exchange for online access to digital content, which includes digital goods, digital services, and access to digital platforms. Furthermore, users enter into such exchanges voluntarily and, in principle, knowingly, since they have the opportunity to read and accept or reject the terms and conditions of the privacy policy regarding the treatment of their personal data. However, for tax purposes, it is currently a subject of debate whether the countries where users are located are entitled to tax the value contributed by users to digital businesses that are tax-resident abroad. This discussion is addressed later in the book. For now, the main takeaway is that multisided digital platforms rely heavily on users, who contribute data and digital content that generates value for the digital businesses and whose allocation of taxing rights is currently contested.

Another tax challenge posed by the network effect is the new value creation paradigm derived from the interaction of different user groups. This paradigm encompasses positive externalities that are captured and monetized by multisided digital platforms. For example, the main source of revenue for many multisided digital platforms derives from the sale of online targeted advertising rather than from the business developed to attracts users, which often is supplied free of charge to generate a base of users. However, the network effect is not limited to user-focused multisided digital platforms that monetize via the sale of online user-targeted advertising or the sale of user-related data and digital content. It is also present in online e-commerce marketplace platforms that act as brokers and monetize by charging a transactional fee for each trade executed between users of the digital platform. In this business model, the network effect is monetized via user transactions rather than via user data. It is important to distinguish clearly both business approaches, although they are not exclusive. Indeed, one digital company may benefit from both simultaneously (Amazon). At the same time,

Table 2.4 Network Effect in Tax-Disruptive Digital Business Models

Tax-disruptive digital business model	Presence of network effect
1. Sale of nonuser digital content	X
2. Licensing of nonuser digital content	X
3. Subscription to nonuser digital content	X
4. Virtual banking	X
5. Virtual insurance	X
6. Online gambling	X
7. Online e-commerce marketplace	✓
8. Sale of user-related data and digital content	✓
9. Online user-targeted advertising	✓
10. Sale of user-related goodwill	✓

Source: Original table for this publication.

the network effect is not common to all digital business models; it is only common to tax-disruptive digital business models that use multisided digital platforms, as shown in table 2.4. The physical or digital nature of the products traded is irrelevant.

Lack of Physical Presence and Scale without Mass

Digital technology allows business to operate in a country without a physical presence. This ability renders the notion of a brick-and-mortar permanent establishment inapplicable and allows digital activities to go untaxed. It poses a significant tax challenge since, traditionally, physical presence has been the main factor used to determine the right of a country to tax foreign businesses generating activity conducted within its borders. In the absence of a physical presence and lack of applicable nexus rules, current tax rules cannot determine the existence of a permanent establishment in the territory, and income generated from digital activities therein goes untaxed. Digital automation and the intangible nature of digital content have facilitated the handling of a growing amount of work or sales in a more cost-effective manner, with zero marginal investment cost, allowing digital businesses to reach scale without mass.

Current initiatives to overcome the limitations of the permanent establishment notion focus on revising traditional nexus rules (box 2.1). However, such efforts should aim to define—not describe—the notion of permanent establishment, as the descriptive approach taken initially has weighed heavily on the effectiveness and evolution of this construct since its inception over a century ago. In other words, defining an idea is not the same as providing examples of such an idea. While the latter may prove easier to understand and more effective in conveying the concept, the former is the only way to build a notion that will stand the test of time and adapt to new realities and tax challenges, such as those posed by the digital economy.

Box 2.1 *South Dakota v. Wayfair*: A New "Economic Nexus"

Even a conservative-dominated United States Supreme Court, in *South Dakota* v. *Wayfair*, has acknowledged the importance of a jurisdiction being able to tax remote sellers (Avi-Yonah 2018; Hellerstein, Owens, and Dimitropoulou 2019). The Wayfair case involves the ability of a state to impose on a remote seller the burden of collecting a state use tax (for which the taxpayer is the in-state purchaser). The constitutional issue in the case was whether this was permitted under the "dormant" commerce clause. The Supreme Court held that it was, and most analysts would agree that the ruling removed the barrier to imposing an income tax on remote sellers. Several states have adopted "economic nexus" standards to impose income tax on remote sellers. While this may seem too forward-leaning and US-centric, in the United States, there apparently is no constitutional barrier to taxing remote sellers under an income tax and, as academic literature recognizes in a reserved tone, the rationale of the Supreme Court in *Wayfair* strongly supports such a tax.

The traditional definition of permanent establishment has focused on the means—whether material (fixed place of business) or personal (dependent agent)—used to conduct the business activity rather than on the business activity itself. The descriptive approach has resulted in a listing of means (physical facilities that constitute a permanent establishment), special situations (building sites), limitations (temporary, independent agents), exclusions (activities of a preparatory or auxiliary character, storage, display, delivery), and special rules (insurance companies) that have turned the permanent establishment notion into a mishmash of examples and exceptions, lacking any sense of cohesion, consistency, and structure. Such examples derive from the German law back in 1932, as reported in the 1932–33 League of Nations' *Report on Taxation of Foreign and National Enterprises* (Carroll 1932, 1933). Nowadays, 90 years later, the list remains unchanged, proving that the notion of permanent establishment has become obsolete and must be reworked to address the tax challenges posed by the digital economy.

As a proposal *de lege ferenda*, a proper definition of permanent establishment should focus on the nature and traits that define the existence of foreign business activity in a territory, to make sure that the definition is not contaminated or limited by historical or factual considerations. The general clause dealing with traditional permanent establishment focuses on the physical nature of the presence and means needed to undertake a business activity. Today, business activity may be carried out remotely, with little or no physical presence in a territory, especially when dealing with digital services. Permanent establishment should be defined based on the traits of a business activity that are considered sufficient to create value in the territory and that are worth being taxed therein, on the premise that the territory is central to the value creation of such business activity. Hence, new digital technologies conduct business in novel ways, and a flexible definition is needed that can adapt the concept of permanent establishment to the new digital economy. Yet, as shown in table 2.5, not all tax-disruptive digital business models would be covered by a revised definition of permanent establishment, since multisided digital platforms do not provide goods or services to users; instead, they only facilitate trade between user groups.

Table 2.5 Scope of Application of a Revised Notion of Permanent Establishment

Tax-disruptive digital business model	Within the scope of a revised notion of permanent establishment
1. Sale of nonuser digital content	✓
2. Licensing of nonuser digital content	✓
3. Subscription to nonuser digital content	✓
4. Virtual banking	✓
5. Virtual insurance	✓
6. Online gambling	✓
7. Online e-commerce marketplace	X
8. Sale of user-related data and digital content	X
9. Online user-targeted advertising	X
10. Sale of user-related goodwill	X

Source: Original table for this publication.

Note

1. This is a variant of the very old tax problem of determining the correct value of goods exchanged (barter) rather than bought and sold in a free market. We fully agree and recognize the intrinsic valuation issues arising from exchanges involving digital content and user data. These exchanges are among the most hard-to-value intangibles, especially since raw data are different from processed data.

Bibliography

Avi-Yonah, Reuven. 2018. "Designing a 21st Century Taxing Threshold: Some International Implications of *South Dakota* vs. *Wayfair.*" Research Paper 611, University of Michigan, Ann Arbor, June 25, 2018.

Bornman, Marina, and Marianne Wassermann. 2020. "Tax Knowledge for the Digital Economy." *Journal of Economic and Financial Sciences* 13 (1): 1–11.

Carroll, Mitchell. 1932. *Report on Taxation of Foreign and National Enterprises: A Study of the Tax Systems and the Methods of Allocation of the Profits of Enterprises Operating in More Than One Country.* Vol. 1. Geneva: League of Nations.

Carroll, Mitchell. 1933. *Report on Taxation of Foreign and National Enterprises: A Study of the Tax Systems and the Methods of Allocation of the Profits of Enterprises Operating in More Than One Country.* Vols. 2 and 3. Geneva: League of Nations.

Chohan, Usman. 2020. "Some Precepts of the Digital Economy." Critical Blockchain Research Initiative (CBRI) Working Paper, Centre for Aerospace and Security Studies (CASS), Islamabad.

Fetzer, Thomas, and Bianka Dinger. 2019. "The Digital Platform Economy and Its Challenges to Taxation." *Tsinghua China Law Review* 12 (29): 30–56.

Gupta, Sanjeev, Michael Keen, Alpa Shah, and Geneviève Verdier. 2017. *Digital Revolutions in Public Finance.* Washington, DC: International Monetary Fund.

Harpaz, Assaf. 2020. "Taxation of the Digital Economy: Adapting a Twentieth-Century Tax System to a Twenty-First Century Economy." *Yale Journal of International Law* 45.

Haslehner, Werner, Georg Kofler, Katerina Pantazatou, and Alexander Rust, eds. 2019. *Tax and the Digital Economy: Challenges and Proposals for Reform.* Series on International Taxation 69. Alphen aan den Rijn: Kluwer Law International.

Hellerstein, Walter, Jeffrey Owens, and Christina Dimitropoulou. 2019. "Digital Taxation Lessons from Wayfair and the U.S. States' Responses." *Tax Notes International* 94: 241.

Krever, Richard. 2000. "Electronic Commerce and Taxation: A Summary of the Emerging Issues." *Asia-Pacific Tax Bulletin* 6 (6): 151–63.

Lessig, Lawrence. 2000. "Code Is Law: On Liberty in Cyberspace." *Harvard Magazine* (January–February): n.p.

Rukundo, Solomon. 2020. "Addressing the Challenges of Taxation of the Digital Economy: Lessons for African Countries." ICTD Working Paper 105, International Centre for Tax and Development, Brighton.

Terada-Hagiwara, Akiko, Kathrina Gonzales, and Jie Wang. 2019. *Taxation Challenges in a Digital Economy: The Case of the People's Republic of China.* Manila: Asian Development Bank.

CHAPTER 3

Tax Principles Applied to Taxing the Digital Economy

Tax principles have traditionally informed and guided the development of tax systems. However, not all tax principles have the same impact on the taxation of the digital economy. For example, vertical equity is normally applied to personal taxation, while the digital economy is business-centered, where progressive taxation is absent. Some tax principles are intended mainly to address tax policy considerations (equity, benefit, neutrality), while others aim to facilitate tax administration (certainty, simplicity, enforceability). Consequently, the former have greater importance than the latter, since, for example, an unfair tax will never be admissible on the basis of its enforceability or its simplicity. Accordingly, this chapter analyzes those tax principles that have a direct impact on taxing the digital economy.

Horizontal Equity

The concept of horizontal equity provides that two taxpayers with equal ability to pay should pay the same amount of tax. It also implies that two taxpayers with similar economic circumstances should receive an equivalent tax treatment. Why is this implication relevant and necessary? Fairness requires treating equally those that are equal and differently those that are different, so the first step is to determine whether two taxpayers are equal or different for tax purposes. As a consequence, before we measure their ability to pay, it is necessary to assess the economic circumstances of the taxpayers and their respective business models. Unless done this way, there is a risk that we might try to apply the horizontal equity principle to taxpayers that do not share similar economic circumstances and that, therefore, are not comparable from a tax perspective. Only once it is established that the taxpayers share similar economic circumstances will their ability to pay and the application of horizontal equity enter into play.

How does the presence of digital elements affect the economic circumstances of taxpayers in terms of their comparability for purposes of applying the horizontal equity principle? In other words, do traditional business models and digital business models share similar economic circumstances? Do traditional business models and tax-disruptive digital business models share similar economic circumstances? What about digital and tax-disruptive digital ones?

The use of digital technology has enabled the appearance of new business models that operate differently from traditional business models. As already discussed, some new business models do not differ excessively from traditional ones (digital business models), while others have introduced features that significantly alter traditional tax practice (tax-disruptive digital business models). In this context, it is crucial to assess how the presence of digital elements has affected the economic circumstances of taxpayers operating business models that are comparable from a business perspective, though potentially different from a tax perspective.

To answer these questions, it is necessary to distinguish digital business models clearly from tax-disruptive digital business models. As seen in chapter 2, digital business models incorporate certain digital elements (communication, payment) that do not significantly alter traditional tax practices: the essential elements of the transaction (content, distribution, automation) continue to be tangible and require a physical presence in the territory. Consequently, digital business models should be considered comparable to their equivalent traditional business models if they share similar economic circumstances: the nexus for tax purposes does not change, given the need for a physical presence in the market jurisdiction. The same should apply to taxpayers that operate such models.

For example, let us consider two companies that sell the same tangible goods, one with a physical store and the other with an online website for processing orders; the former accepts cash payments, while the latter only processes credit card payments. In principle, both companies conduct an equivalent business activity and share similar economic circumstances, since both businesses require similar infrastructure in terms of inventory, storage, handling, and distribution. The only exception is the presence the physical store, which is a business decision, since alternative nondigital communication channels are available to publicize the business activity (printed yellow pages, infomercials and shopping channels, word of mouth), as traditionally used to commercialize tangible goods and services. Both businesses may opt to outsource any or all of the value chain functions (production, storage, delivery, customer service), irrespective of whether or not they use digital communication or digital payment; outsourcing is irrelevant for tax purposes as long as the business activity involves a physical presence in the territory. Even more, many companies conduct their business by simultaneously operating through both a physical store and an online website, since the digital presence has become an additional communication channel.

Each type of tax-disruptive digital business model must be analyzed separately to determine if it is comparable to its equivalent traditional business model, meaning that they share similar economic circumstances. As explained, tax-disruptive digital businesses are characterized by the lack of a physical presence in the market jurisdictions where they operate, which is facilitated by the digital nature of all of their elements. However, the tax-disruptive character of these business models arises from the intangible nature of the content, the automation, and the distribution, which enable the lack of a physical presence in terms of product, labor, and delivery.

More precisely, the intangible nature of the content, apart from escaping traditional customs controls, eliminates any need for storage facilities given the absence of physical inventories,[1] which has an impact on a firm's economic circumstances. Such savings are offset by the additional investment required to develop the product technology, which may cost even more to develop than its equivalent tangible product (for example, the cost of developing the technology for e-books may well exceed the cost of printing paper books). The savings from digital automation also lower the costs of hiring labor and having a workforce physically present in the territory. Since processes are digitally automated, human intervention is reduced to a minimum, which precludes the need for either physical premises (factories, stores, storage facilities) or dependent agents or employees (who are replaced by digitally automated processes). Finally, the online distribution channel allows the delivery of digital content without the need for physical infrastructure (transportation, physical stores, delivery providers, logistics contractors, postal mail services), which renders untraceable by means of traditional monitoring the delivery of digital content to online customers in market jurisdictions. As with digital content and digital automation, this new online distribution channel entails a significant cost to develop the technological infrastructure needed to distribute the automated content digitally, which adds to the disconnect in economic circumstances. Therefore, the presence of digital elements, like content, automation, and distribution, has an impact on the economic circumstances of tax-disruptive digital business models as compared to their equivalent traditional ones.

The impact of such digital elements may differ from one tax-disruptive digital business model to another, when compared to their respective equivalent traditional business models. The tax-disruptive trait of digital elements is their lack of physical presence—that is, their intangible nature—but not all digital elements have an impact on the economic circumstances of taxpayers (digital communication, digital payment). However, content may be intangible due to either its digital nature (e-book) or its own nature (intermediation services, user data, customer lists, goodwill), independent of the tangible nature of the support used to communicate or distribute it (optical discs, paper format). Accordingly, some tax-disruptive digital business models may share similar economic circumstances with their equivalent traditional business models when the role of digital elements is merely accessory to the unique, intangible nature of the content. For example, data can be transmitted and shared in writing, online, or over the phone, but its defining intangible trait prevails. The same applies to goodwill, irrespective of how it originates, and to intermediation services, which connect people, whether done in person or online through a multisided platform. Sometimes, the unifying intangible nature of content prevails over the tax-disruptive digital nature of the other elements.

It is necessary to analyze each type of tax-disruptive digital business model to assess whether the economic circumstances are significantly altered by the digital nature of its content, automation, and distribution in comparison to its equivalent traditional business model. To begin with, taxpayers that sell nonuser digital content face different economic circumstances than taxpayers that sell tangible goods and services, especially with regard to physical presence (business premises, workforce, labor costs) and investment costs (technology development costs, digital infrastructure maintenance). For example, as a product, an e-book bears little similarity to a printed book, and their respective underlying economic business structures differ greatly. However, a bookseller may commercialize only printed books through both online and physical channels, in which case the business structure will be common or very similar since the product is the same (and requires inventory, storage, and physical delivery); the website will be simply an additional channel through which to commercialize the product and process orders.

Accordingly, the tax-disruptive digital business model that sells nonuser digital content does not share similar economic circumstances with either its equivalent traditional or its digital business model; it must be treated differently when applying the horizontal equity principle to taxpayers operating under a tax-disruptive digital business model. The same is true about both digital content licensing and subscription models, with the only difference being that, instead of transferring full ownership of the content, these tax-disruptive models only transfer limited rights of use (license, rental). The content itself is entirely different from the tangible version of the product in the respective equivalent traditional business models. For example, let us compare an internet-based video-streaming subscription model (Netflix, Hulu, Disney+) to either a traditional business model like a video rental physical shop (Blockbuster Video) or a digital business model like a DVD-by-mail service that processes orders via a website (as Netflix started). Both traditional and digital business models rent physical DVDs that require inventory, storage, and physical delivery, while the internet video-streaming business model provides online access to digital content without any need for physical support or presence in the market country. Likewise, the tax-disruptive digital business model that licenses digital content (Microsoft Office online access, McAfee antivirus online protection) is not similar in economic circumstances to its traditional business model (packaged software distributed through physical stores or ordered online and physically delivered). To summarize, taxpayers conducting tax-disruptive digital business models involving the sale, licensing, or subscription-based access to digital content must be treated differently, for purposes of the horizontal equity principle, from taxpayers selling, licensing, or renting tangible goods and services under both traditional and digital business models.

The tax-disruptive digital business models of virtual banking, virtual insurance, and online banking have in common that they are usually heavily regulated by local authorities, which require special permissions and impose enhanced mechanisms of control. As a result, monitoring of these regulated sectors is reinforced, including from a tax perspective. In horizontal equity terms, all three models differ substantially from their respective equivalent traditional business models in the lack of a physical presence to conduct such activities, which has an impact on their economic circumstances. As an example, traditional gambling facilities (physical casinos, betting shops, bingo halls, physical slot machines) require costly workforce (security personnel, croupiers and dealers, maintenance staff) and have to manage greater risks (handling huge amounts of cash, restricting access to adult players, monitoring cheating practices) than online gambling businesses have to manage. However, some of these cost savings are compensated by the risks of cybercrime that affect these sectors, including banking and insurance, and any online business that processes a high volume of financial transactions. Both virtual banking and insurance businesses are substantially different from traditional banking and insurance businesses, since the lack of a physical presence has an impact on their economic circumstances. Their workforce has been replaced by digitally automated processes, such as the use of robo-advisers that provide automated algorithm-driven financial planning services with little to no human supervision, application of artificial intelligence in risk management for insurance purposes, and use of data mining and big data analysis to improve risk measurement and financial returns.

Furthermore, all three industries are highly dependent on aleatory contracts, where an uncertain event determines the parties' rights and obligations. For example, banking depends on the uncertain returns of investment portfolios, gambling depends on the odds of the bets placed, and insurance depends on whether uncertain events will occur at all or when certain events will occur. Traditionally, such activities required actively soliciting business by directly asking potential customers, either through employees in physical premises (bank branches, casinos, insurance offices) or through the services of dependent agents (commissionaires, insurance sales representatives). In both cases, the businesses would be considered to have a taxable presence in the market jurisdiction, either as an incorporated entity or as a permanent establishment. The virtual nature of these tax-disruptive digital business models has significantly altered their economic circumstances, which are very different.

As refers to tax-disruptive digital business models that benefit from the network effect, which were analyzed in chapter 2, such models have in common that their economic circumstances, in comparison to their equivalent traditional business models, are not affected significantly by the lack of a physical presence, given that their content is intangible by its very nature (user data, intermediation services, customer lists, goodwill), irrespective of the digital nature or not of the business model. In other words, traditional business models that involve any of these intangible contents should be considered to share similar economic circumstances with their equivalent tax-disruptive digital business models. For example, business models based on user-related data share the same content as traditional businesses conducting public polls and public surveys, with the differentiating factor being the method of obtaining such data (online processing of automated data versus collection of data in person or by telephone). Moreover, all business models use the data obtained for similar purposes (user-targeted advertising, sale of user-related goodwill, sale of user data). Likewise, online marketplaces offer intermediary services that traditionally were offered via alternative venues (trade fairs, trade exhibitions, industry conventions, brokerage firms). In any case, the value of the business model lies in the networking effect, which is intangible by nature and has a minor impact on the economic circumstances of the taxpayers conducting such businesses in either form, digital or not.

Table 3.1 summarizes the similarity of economic circumstances between taxpayers conducting different types of business models, in order to assess whether they should be treated as equals or not when applying horizontal equity.

Thus, businesses that share similar economic circumstances should be assessed on their ability to pay against a common benchmark—that is, they should be subject to the same tax regime, irrespective of their digital nature or not, and should be taxed equally whenever they have similar ability to pay. The taxation of these new business models is addressed in the analysis of the neutrality principle. The taxation of tax-disruptive digital business models that are different in economic circumstances from their equivalent traditional business models is addressed in the analysis of the benefit principle.

Benefit Principle

In the absence of a physical nexus between companies operating tax-disruptive digital business models and their market jurisdictions, an alternative tax principle could justify the existence of taxing rights of market jurisdictions over the proceeds derived from their operations therein: the benefit principle. Not all taxes are based on ability to pay. For instance, governments may impose taxes on resident and nonresident companies that derive a benefit from the goods and services they provide. This practice is known as the benefit principle of taxation, which holds that tax burdens should be assigned according to the benefits that taxpayers receive from government goods and services, which can be specific or general in nature. While this principle is more obvious for individual taxpayers, who benefit from government services like health, education, police, fire, or defense protection, it is also relevant for corporate taxpayers, which benefit from advantageous and operational legal structures for the proper functioning of their

Table 3.1 Comparison of Economic Circumstances of Business Models

Digital or tax-disruptive digital business model	*Do operators share similar economic circumstances as those using equivalent traditional business models?*
Digital business models (all types)	✓
Tax-disruptive digital business models	
1. Sale of nonuser digital content	X
2. Licensing of nonuser digital content	X
3. Subscription to nonuser digital content	X
4. Virtual banking	X
5. Virtual insurance	X
6. Online gambling	X
7. Online e-commerce marketplace	✓
8. Sale of user-related data and digital content	✓
9. Online user-targeted advertising	✓
10. Sale of user-related goodwill	✓

Source: Original table for this publication.

business—for example, in the form of a stable legal and regulatory environment, protection of intellectual property and the knowledge-based capital of the firm, enforcement of consumer protection laws, or well-developed transportation, telecommunication, utilities, and other infrastructure.

However, the range of benefits varies widely among businesses depending on their residence status, since tax-resident companies derive much greater benefits from their governments than do nonresident companies operating in a given territory. Even assuming that countries potentially offer the same benefits to all businesses irrespective of their tax-residence status, the exercise of the corresponding rights is significantly more burdensome and costly for nonresident companies, to the point that the effective benefits derived by nonresidents may well go unnoticed. Thus, a new distinction must be introduced into the analysis: resident versus nonresident tax-disruptive digital businesses. Mere digital businesses require a physical presence in their market jurisdictions that automatically creates a nexus for tax-residence purposes (in the form of a permanent establishment), while tax-disruptive digital businesses may operate their entire value chain without having any physical presence in the market country, even when the digital supplier is a tax resident. As a consequence, as also happens in transfer pricing, it is necessary to distinguish between the domestic and international digital economy, since digital transactions may originate within or across borders, depending on whether the digital supplier is a tax resident in the market jurisdiction or somewhere else.

For purposes of applying the benefit principle, two parameters are relevant when assessing the benefit derived by legal entities:

- *Degree of physical presence*. Businesses involving tangible products and using physical facilities benefit more from physical infrastructure, like transportation or utilities, than businesses involving intangible content by nature, like software or digital advertising companies.
- *Tax-residence status*. Tax-resident companies benefit more from the legal structure and protection offered by their government than nonresident businesses effectively do.

Accordingly, the benefit assessment may range from a minimum in the case of nonresident entities operating tax-disruptive digital business models to a maximum in the case of resident companies operating traditional and digital business models. In between, both nonresident entities operating traditional and digital business models as well as resident companies operating tax-disruptive digital business models benefit from different government goods and services. Table 3.2 summarizes the extent to which different types of business models benefit from government goods and services based on their tax residence. As shown, benefits may refer, on the one hand, to legal structure and protection of rights and, on the other hand, to a more tangible dimension, including physical infrastructure and property protection. The former is applicable to all resident businesses, while the latter is limited to companies operating business models that require a physical presence.

Table 3.2 Scope of Benefit, by Type of Business Model and Tax Residence

Type of business model	Is the business a tax resident?	Benefits received by companies from government	
		Legal environment	*Physical infrastructure*
Tax-disruptive	No	X	X
Regulated	No	✓/X	X
Digital	No	X	✓
Traditional	No	X	✓
Tax-disruptive	Yes	✓	X
Regulated	Yes	✓	X
Digital	Yes	✓	✓
Traditional	Yes	✓	✓

Source: Original table for this publication.

Most companies operating tax-disruptive digital business models obtain no benefit from the foreign governments of market jurisdictions where they operate. In the first place, they do not benefit from physical infrastructure given their intangible nature. For example, digital content does not require any transportation infrastructure, any police, fire, or defense protection, or any utilities (water supply, gas supply). Yet foreign tax-disruptive digital companies do benefit from physical infrastructure in the market jurisdiction (fiber optic network, power grid). However, such physical infrastructure is often privately owned,[2] which means that such benefits are not provided by the government, but instead are contracted and paid for by the tax-disruptive digital business and its users, acting as customers.

This consideration is very important. The benefit principle focuses on benefits derived by entities from governments, not from companies or individuals located in the market jurisdiction, since governments do not own such companies or individuals. This point is relevant because, in tax-disruptive digital business models, users contribute data and content in exchange for access to digital content and digital platforms that is supplied free of charge but has a cost for the provider. In this regard, it has been argued that market jurisdictions might have a claim over taxing rights on the basis of the value contributed by users in the form of data and content. Nevertheless, such user contributions are not made for free. Instead, businesses provide in-kind compensation to users in the form of free access to digital content and platforms for which users would otherwise have to pay. Therefore, tax-disruptive digital businesses do not obtain any unpaid benefit from users and even less from governments of market jurisdictions. Consequently, such claims of market jurisdictions over taxing rights cannot be justified on the basis of the benefit principle, despite any market asymmetries.

Finally, nonresident businesses do not draw any benefits from the legal environment in market jurisdictions, since, apart from the already mentioned difficulties of exercising and enforcing their rights (costly access to judicial system, burdensome bureaucracy to enforce foreign court decisions, expensive discovery pretrial procedures), the legal and regulatory framework, including enforcement of consumer protection laws, imposes duties and obligations on companies rather than providing them with benefits; the rationale behind those norms is to protect consumers rather than businesses. In addition, intellectual property protection is not granted on a general basis to any company; it is only granted to those that have previously filed for such protection, upon payment of substantial filing fees in each jurisdiction where they seek legal protection.

Notwithstanding the above, there is an exception to the lack of benefit that nonresident businesses draw from the legal environment in market jurisdictions: the case of companies conducting business in regulated sectors (banking, insurance, gambling). Nonresident entities operating such tax-disruptive digital business models do benefit from legal and regulatory protection in the jurisdictions where they operate because they must fulfill the mandatory procedures and requirements to be legally authorized to conduct such activity therein. Still, nonresident entities may attempt to operate without the appropriate authorization in the territory, by taking undue advantage of the lack of a physical presence and the added difficulty of detection by the legal authorities. In this case, legal action should be taken.

However, tax-resident entities, irrespective of their business models, enjoy the benefits of the legal environment of their residence country, which in this case is the same as the market jurisdiction where they operate. These benefits are associated with the notion of tax residence, which entitles tax-resident businesses to benefit from tax treaty provisions that provide relief from double taxation, whenever they operate in foreign market jurisdictions that apply source taxation. There is no doubt about the right to tax resident entities on the basis of the benefit principle. Additionally, the same resident entities whose businesses involve a physical presence in the territory— basically taxpayers operating traditional and digital business models—should bear higher taxes than taxpayers that operate tax-disruptive digital businesses, which do not benefit from the physical infrastructure provided by governments, if any at all, given their intangible nature and their lack of a physical presence.

From the analysis of the benefit principle, we must conclude that nonresident entities conducting business in a market jurisdiction through a tax-disruptive digital business model should not be subject to taxation in such territory because they do not derive any benefits from its government. The exception is those companies developing business activities in regulated sectors like banking, insurance, and gambling, which derive benefits to the extent that the government of the market jurisdiction provides legal protection of the regulated activity; otherwise, such nonresident companies in regulated sectors should not be taxed. Finally, in accordance with the benefit principle, nonresident digital businesses should be taxed in the same manner as their equivalent nonresident traditional businesses, since they derive similar benefits from physical infrastructure, as long as it is government owned.

Neutrality Principle

According to the neutrality principle (also referred to as efficiency), taxes should neither distort economic decisions nor interfere with the investment and spending decisions of businesses and workers. In this regard, tax policies that systematically favor one kind of economic activity over another can lead to the misallocation of resources or, worse, to schemes whose only purpose is to exploit such preferential tax treatment. If individuals or businesses make their investment or spending decisions based on the tax code rather than on their own preferences, then the tax system fails to meet the neutrality principle and could lead to negative economic consequences in the long run.

As concluded from the analysis of the horizontal equity principle, businesses that share similar economic circumstances should be assessed on their ability to pay against a common benchmark—that is, they should be subject to the same tax regime, irrespective of their digital nature or not, and taxed equally whenever they have similar ability to pay. In this context, both digital business models and tax-disruptive digital business models where a network effect is present, all of which share similar economic circumstances to their respective equivalent traditional business models (as shown in table 3.1), should be taxed by reference to their equivalent traditional business models, without taking into account the presence of any digital elements. The rationale behind this approach is that when two comparable business models have the same commercial result, they should have the same tax result. Commercial decisions on the structuring of transactions and business models should not be distorted by tax considerations.

In contrast, the neutrality principle only applies to comparable business models that share similar economic circumstances, which excludes from its scope those tax-disruptive digital business models that differ significantly from their equivalent traditional business models (table 3.1). Hence, such tax-disruptive digital business models should be taxed differently than their equivalent traditional business models, since the presence of certain digital elements (content, automation, distribution) makes them substantially different and requires separate tax treatment. As a consequence, the taxation of these tax-disruptive digital business models should be designed on the basis of other tax principles, such as the benefit principle or the source taxation principle, assuming that the business entities are not tax residents in the market jurisdiction. Obviously, all tax-resident companies operating digital and tax-disruptive digital business models should be taxed as any other resident corporate taxpayer, although additional tax monitoring and enforcement mechanisms may be needed.

It is as discriminatory to breach neutrality when taxing companies that share similar economic circumstances as it is to apply the same taxation to businesses that are significantly different from the perspective of horizontal equity. The basis of a fair tax system is treating those that are equal equally and treating those that are different differently. First, as already analyzed, the economic circumstances of business models need to be compared to determine whether horizontal equity is met. Next, the ability to pay of those that are comparable needs to be assessed against a common benchmark, specifically the tax regime applicable to the traditional business model, in compliance with the neutrality principle. Finally, once the ability to pay is assessed, the same taxation should be imposed on those businesses with equal ability to pay, irrespective of the presence of digital elements, in compliance with the horizontal equity principle.

Taxation of tax-disruptive digital business models that are not comparable to their equivalent traditional business models in terms of horizontal equity should be determined in accordance with alternative tax principles, like the benefit principle or source taxation principle. Consequently, tax principles are interconnected and complement each other.

Those digital and tax-disruptive digital business models to which the neutrality principle is applicable should be taxed the same as their equivalent traditional business models.[3] As already said, focus should be on nonresident companies, since resident ones should be subject to taxation on the basis of tax residence, irrespective of their physical presence in the territory (any company considered a tax resident in a territory will be subject to taxation in that territory, without the need for an additional nexus).

Accordingly, nonresident companies operating digital business models without a permanent establishment in the market jurisdiction should be taxed like nonresident companies operating equivalent traditional business models, if and whenever they are taxed in the absence of a permanent establishment. For example, in general, nonresident (in the market jurisdiction) companies operating traditional business models consisting of nondigital transactions (phone sales, postal orders) involving the physical supply of goods or services using traditional payment methods are not taxable in the market jurisdiction, unless a permanent establishment is considered to exist there. As a consequence, based on application of the neutrality principle, nonresident companies operating digital business models without a permanent establishment in the market jurisdiction should not be subject to taxation in the market jurisdiction, in the absence of a valid applicable nexus in accordance with traditional tax principles. The opposite would violate the existing and long-standing tax principles on which worldwide tax systems are based and currently operate at an international level.

Nonresident companies operating tax-disruptive digital business models where the network effect is present (online e-commerce marketplace, sale of user-related data and digital content, online user-targeted advertising, sale of user-related goodwill) should be taxed like nonresident companies operating equivalent traditional business models, if and whenever they are taxed in the absence of a permanent establishment in the market jurisdiction. For example, nonresident (in the market jurisdiction) companies operating traditional business models consisting of nondigital transactions that monetize intangibles such as advertising rights, intermediation services, user data, customer lists, or goodwill (telephone survey companies offering phone market research, customer survey services, and customer service satisfaction surveys; media brokers and advisers for media agencies acting as wholesalers of advertising space; commodity brokerage firms) are not taxable in the market jurisdiction, unless a permanent establishment is considered to exist there. As a consequence, based on application of the neutrality principle, nonresident companies operating tax-disruptive digital business models where the network effect is present, but lacking a permanent establishment in the market jurisdiction, should not be subject to taxation in the market jurisdiction, in the absence of a valid applicable nexus in accordance with traditional tax principles (table 3.3). Once again, the opposite would violate the existing and long-standing tax principles on which worldwide tax systems are based and currently operate at an international level.

Table 3.3 Taxable Digital Business Models Based on the Neutrality Principle

Companies operating digital business models that are taxable based on the neutrality principle	*Resident*	Nonresident	
		Permanent establishment	*No permanent establishment*
Digital business models (all types)	✓	✓	X
Tax-disruptive digital business models			
7. Online e-commerce marketplace	✓	✓	X
8. Sale of user-related data and digital content	✓	✓	X
9. Online user-targeted advertising	✓	✓	X
10. Sale of user-related goodwill	✓	✓	X

Source: Original table for this publication.

The domestic digital economy comprises digital transactions carried out in a market jurisdiction by tax-resident companies or permanent establishments of nonresident entities. The neutrality principle should be taken into account when taxing this domestic digital activity.[4] In this respect, the use of tax thresholds and safe harbors should be avoided, to prevent behaviors like fragmentation and other tax avoidance schemes aimed only at unduly escaping taxation. Similarly, granting tax incentives to certain digital activities or business models may result in companies maneuvering to exploit such advantageous tax treatment, which clashes with the main purpose of the neutrality principle: to prevent taxes from distorting businesses decisions.

Finally, by way of summary, based on the benefit and neutrality tax principles, companies operating digital and tax-disruptive digital business models at a domestic level should be taxed like companies operating the equivalent traditional business models, while companies operating without any physical presence in the market jurisdiction should be taxed in their country of tax residence.

Tax Sovereignty

Taxation has always been a key feature of state sovereignty. However, the digital economy may pose a new threat to tax sovereignty in the form of additional competitive pressure on the part of other jurisdictions that claim new taxing rights. More specifically, market jurisdictions where foreign digital companies operate without any physical presence have started to claim new taxing rights over the proceeds arising from digital activity conducted within their borders. These jurisdictions argue that value is created within their territory and that digital companies benefit from data and content contributed by users located in the market jurisdictions. Based on this view, these countries are attempting to create new taxing rights and to establish new nexus and profit allocation rules that may justify their claims of additional taxing rights over the proceeds obtained by foreign digital companies (digital services taxes, equalization levies, significant economic presence). Indeed, some countries have already introduced unilateral tax measures along these lines.

This section analyzes whether these claims from market jurisdictions may be validated by traditional tax theory. Tax sovereignty refers to the power of states to tax their citizenry and their territory, which is the basis for residence taxation and source taxation, respectively. Historically, the rationale for residence taxation has been that the state of residence provides certain facilities and services (benefits) to its residents. In contrast, the justification for source taxation has been that the source state makes the generation of income possible. It has already been established that companies operating digital and tax-disruptive digital business models are taxable in their state of residence on their worldwide income on the basis of residence taxation, unless a territorial system applies. Similarly, permanent establishments of nonresident entities operating digital and tax-disruptive digital business models are taxable in the market jurisdiction, which is also the source state, on their local income on the basis of source taxation.

The question becomes whether market jurisdictions have grounds to tax nonresident companies operating digital and tax-disruptive digital business models without a physical presence in their territories. This question leads to our previous analysis, which we summarize here. Obviously, these market jurisdictions cannot tax nonresident companies on the basis of residence taxation; the only other option is to claim taxing rights on the basis of source taxation. Source taxation is justified by the view that the country that provides the opportunity to generate income should have the right to tax it. However, without any physical presence or any benefits derived from the source state, the only argument left to justify the tax claim over the proceeds of nonresident digital companies is to consider the local users who contribute data and content as part of the source state. This argument should not be accepted given that people are not the property of anyone and do not belong to any state. Governments cannot misappropriate data and content generated by users and treat them as government benefits provided to nonresidents, especially when they have not contributed to generating such data or digital content. Moreover, many of those users may not even be citizens or tax residents of such market jurisdictions (tourists who consume digital content while on vacation).

Even more, it is important to remember that such users do not contribute data and content for free. Businesses provide in-kind compensation to users in the form of free access to digital content and platforms that users would otherwise need to pay for to obtain. Therefore, tax-disruptive digital businesses obtain no unpaid benefit from users and even less benefit from governments of market jurisdictions. Additionally, the economic value of user contributions is widely contested, since, in most instances, raw data and digital content cannot be monetized straight ahead. Instead, the real value for the digital businesses lies in the methodology and technology used to process the data by means of their proprietary digital automation technologies (data storage, data mining, data analytics, data visualization) in order to extract marketable information (user-based segmentation data sets) that can be monetized. As we have seen, the majority of digital and tax-disruptive digital business models do not even benefit from data and content contributed by users (online sale, licensing, and subscription of nonuser digital content; online regulated activities like banking, insurance, or gambling), which automatically discards such justification. For these reasons, source taxation cannot be applied to such nonresident business models.

Another reason that supports the allocation of exclusive taxing rights to the state of residence—therefore impeding any claims from foreign market jurisdictions—is the issue of tax losses generated by failed digital businesses. Such tax losses are borne by the state of residence, especially if the resident digital company is part of a consolidated group of enterprises, which allows such tax losses to be offset against the profits of other group entities. Assuming that the digital company goes out of business before making any profit, only tax losses are left for the state of residence, which endures the tax sacrifice from failed digital businesses without sharing it with market jurisdictions. This situation is similar to what happens with failed lines of research in the pharmaceutical industry.

Administrative Feasibility

Based on the analysis of tax principles, nonresident companies operating digital and tax-disruptive digital business models in a territory without a permanent establishment should not be taxed on their proceeds by the market jurisdiction. Yet the digital economy comprises digital transactions that can be subject to taxation not only from the side of the digital supplier but also from the side of the digital user who is located in the market jurisdiction. Therefore, most digital transactions are taxable in market jurisdictions by way of indirect taxation that, quite often, is ultimately borne by users located in the territory where the digital consumption takes place.

Indeed, indirect taxation of the digital economy is internationally accepted, with the Organisation for Economic Co-operation and Development having issued international guidelines and other materials related to the value added tax (VAT) and goods and services tax (GST) (OECD 2017a, 2017b, 2019) and countries increasingly expanding the scope of indirect taxes (VAT/GST) to digital supplies. Additional efforts are also being invested in developing mechanisms for the effective collection of VAT/GST where the supplier is not located in the jurisdiction of taxation (the market jurisdiction) as well as in defining the role of digital platforms in the collection of VAT/GST on online sales. Moreover, business-to-consumer (B2C) digital transactions involve an additional layer of complexity for tax administration purposes, since nonresident digital suppliers or tax agents (digital platforms) are responsible for collecting the VAT/GST from users and for remitting the taxes collected to the tax administrations of market jurisdictions where those users are located. This creates opportunities for tax evasion if the nonresident digital supplier contravenes the obligation to register for VAT/GST in a market jurisdiction and chooses to keep the taxes collected. Exploiting the lack of physical presence and the intangible nature of the goods and services rendered in the territory makes it very difficult to monitor and identify such digital activity.

Although the same risk exists for domestic digital transactions involving resident digital suppliers, monitoring and enforcement mechanisms of tax administrations are more effective when dealing with resident entities, in terms of both access to information and enforcement measures (seizing property, freezing accounts). Indeed, taxpayers do not fear tax audits; taxpayers fear effective tax enforcement, which ultimately may have two types of consequences: loss of assets (property and funds seized) and loss of freedom (imprisonment); both have a greater deterrent effect in the country where assets are located and individuals are present (corporate officers and directors).

With regard to domestic digital transactions, from the side of the digital supplier, not only is the collection of indirect taxes at risk, but so is the direct taxation of both resident digital suppliers and permanent establishments of nonresident entities. This risk is a consequence of the added difficulty derived from the intangible nature of digital content, which escapes the traditional monitoring techniques used by tax administrations. Furthermore, although tax evasion is widespread and existed long before digital technology appeared, digital elements of transactions have introduced new disruptive aspects that require specific measures to tackle tax evasion arising from digital transactions. Moreover, tax evasion is not exclusively a domestic issue; indeed, it is quite the opposite. While there are domestic tax evasion schemes that benefit from digital technology, the majority of tax evasion schemes in digital transactions involve nonresident suppliers.

For example, digital transactions could be tracked via digital payments. Although some digital payments do not require the intervention of traditional financial institutions (cryptocurrencies, virtual currencies, stored-value cards), the majority of digital payments are channeled through banks and credit card companies. Most internet users still earn their income outside the internet, so their salary payments are channeled through banks in traditional ways. Only users whose economy relies exclusively on digital payment methods outside the traditional financial sector may escape such financial sector control. Unfortunately, the financial sector is not always eager to collaborate in tax enforcement tasks (applying withholding to their customers), because they fear losing clients to financial institutions located abroad that do not abide by the same national legal obligations or simply are not subject to them. As a consequence, any effort undertaken in this direction should be at the global level, well beyond national boundaries and local legislations.

Tax policy principles (horizontal equity, benefit, neutrality, tax sovereignty) must always prevail over tax administration considerations (certainty, simplicity, enforceability),[5] even if the tax policy is rendered unenforceable. The use of rebuttable presumptions is relevant in the case of presumptive taxes (turnover taxes). Taxpayers need to have an opportunity to provide adequate evidence that supports accurate and fair taxation: they should be allowed to submit accounting and financial documentation to show their net income and claim a refund, if appropriate, of amounts withheld on account of revenue-based taxes like recent turnover taxes on digital businesses. The trade-off between tax accuracy and administrative feasibility must always be resolved in favor of the former, as long as taxpayers cooperate and provide supporting evidence.

Certainty and simplicity are other important tax administration principles that should be taken into account when designing tax measures to address the digital economy. Tax rules should specify clearly how the amount of tax is assessed so that taxpayers can comply in a cost-efficient manner and governments can easily monitor and enforce taxes. Proposals to tax the digital economy should avoid any unnecessary complexity in the tax assessment, especially in the profit allocation rules (scope of profit subject to taxing right, method for calculating and allocating profit, treatment of losses). Ultimately, the effectiveness of any tax is constrained by the capacity of tax administrations to enforce it. Indeed, the majority of market jurisdictions are low-tax-capacity countries, which demands that any tax initiative be aligned with their tax practices and available resources. Otherwise, only high-capacity countries will be able to implement these initiatives effectively, increasing the gap between countries.

To conclude, figure 3.1 summarizes the interplay of tax principles as applied to digital and tax-disruptive digital business models. As shown, the horizontal equity principle serves as the backbone of tax design theory and as the unifying axis under which the remaining tax principles fulfill their various functions and missions. Accordingly, the first step is to analyze any given digital business model against its equivalent traditional business model to assess whether they share similar economic circumstances. If they do, then they are considered equal for tax purposes. Assuming that they have a similar ability to pay, they should bear the same amount of tax, which is achieved at a subsequent stage by applying to the digital business model the same tax regime as is applied

Figure 3.1 Interaction of Tax Principles as Applied to Digital Business Models

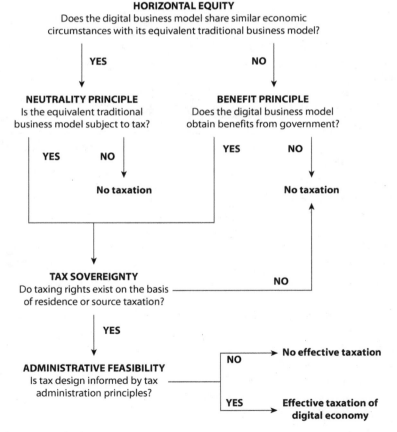

Source: Original figure for this publication.

to the traditional business model. This choice of taxation must be governed by the neutrality principle in order to prevent any discrimination between taxpayers that are deemed to be equal. It must also be based on either residence or source taxation. Hence, if the traditional business model is subject to tax, the same taxation should apply to the digital business model. If no taxation applies to the traditional business model, no tax should be imposed on the digital business model.

If taxation of the digital business model is deemed appropriate, then administrative feasibility principles should inform the design of the digital tax. If business models do not share similar economic circumstances, then the equivalent traditional business model should not be used as a benchmark to determine the taxation of the digital business model, and the benefit principle should be used to assess whether any benefits are derived from the government. In the absence of benefits, no taxation should be imposed, unless residence taxation is applicable on the basis of tax sovereignty, in which case, administrative feasibility considerations should be taken into account.

Notes

1. Although no inventory storage facilities are required for the product (digital content, digital goods, digital services), digital business models require specific and huge electronic infrastructure (server farms), which involves significant investment and maintenance costs that need to be considered.

2. Some scholars have correctly pointed out that physical infrastructure may sometimes be publicly owned, and service may be provided at subsidized costs. Thus, it is not always clear that governments provide no net benefit. Digital businesses may also benefit from the presence of consumers who are receiving subsidized services. In situations where either the infrastructure is publicly owned or the service is subsidized by the government, tax-disruptive digital business models will derive a public benefit.

3. Some scholars have a different view and consider that the critical element of the neutrality principle is the baseline used. They think that the essential element is substitutability. For them, neutrality is important to the extent that taxation alone pushes someone into an alternative that would not be adopted absent the tax. They think that this is a broad standard: the narrower the baseline used, the greater the risk of unintended effects. Consequently, they consider that differentiating tax-disruptive models from other models by definition increases the risk of discrimination and reduces the importance of neutrality.

4. In the *Wayfair* case, described in box 2.1 in chapter 2, the United States Supreme Court's decision was strongly motivated by its view that South Dakota's approach would advance the objective of nondiscrimination by creating a level playing field between in-state and out-of-state traders selling to local purchasers. Some scholars have stressed the true global importance of *Wayfair* for endorsing new nexus rules embodying a virtual presence that reflects the economic reality.

5. Some scholars have expressed reservations about this statement, since they consider that, in a very real sense, tax administration is the same as tax policy in low- and middle-income countries. We agree with their position, but the scope of our analysis is not limited to low- and middle-income countries; it encompasses all countries. The world is not two-dimensional: low- and middle-income countries versus high-income countries. Viewing countries as being in one camp or the other has real limitations.

Bibliography

Cazorla Prieto, Luis María. 2002. *El derecho financiero y tributario en la ciencia jurídica.* Madrid: Editorial Aranzadi.

Einaudi, Luigi. 1938. "La scienza italiana e la imposta ottima." In *Miti e paradossi della giustizia tributaria,* edited by Giulio Einaudi, ch. 10. Torino: Einaudi Editore.

Fleming, Clifton, Robert Peroni, and Stephen Shay. 2001. "Fairness in International Taxation: The Ability-to-Pay Case for Taxing Worldwide Income." *Florida Tax Review* 5 (4): 299–354.

Fleming, Clifton, Robert Peroni, and Stephen Shay. 2008. "Some Perspectives from the United States on the Worldwide Taxation vs. Territorial Taxation Debate." *Journal of the Australasian Tax Teachers Association* 3 (2): 35–86.

Kaplow, Louis. 1989. "Horizontal Equity: Measures in Search of a Principle." *National Tax Journal* 42 (June): 139–54.

Mirrlees, James, Stuart Adam, Tim Besley, Richard Blundell, Stephen Bond, Robert Chote, Malcolm Gammie, Paul Johnson, Gareth Myles, and James M. Poterba. 2011. *Tax by Design: The Mirrlees Review.* Oxford: Oxford University Press.

Musgrave, Richard. 1986. "The Nature of Horizontal Equity and the Principle of Broad-Based Taxation: A Friendly Critique." In *Public Finance in a Democratic Society: The Foundations of Taxation and Expenditure,* vol. 3, ch. 9. New York: New York University Press.

OECD (Organisation for Economic Co-operation and Development). 2017a. "International VAT/GST Guidelines." OECD, Paris, April 12, 2017.

OECD (Organisation for Economic Co-operation and Development). 2017b. "Mechanisms for the Effective Collection of VAT/GST Where the Supplier Is Not Located in the Jurisdiction of Taxation." OECD, Paris.

OECD (Organisation for Economic Co-operation and Development). 2019. "The Role of Digital Platforms in the Collection of VAT/GST on Online Sales." OECD, Paris, March.

Sáinz de Bujanda, Fernando. 1970. "Los métodos de determinación de las bases imponibles y su proyección sobre la estructura del sistema tributario." Lecture delivered at the Real Academia de Jurisprudencia y Legislación, Madrid.

CHAPTER 4

Economic and Legal Issues of Taxing the Digital Economy

Current initiatives for taxing the digital economy may have adverse consequences, which need to be analyzed before making any policy decision. For example, new taxing rights claimed by market jurisdictions (Amount A of the Unified Approach of the Organisation for Economic Co-operation and Development [OECD], turnover-based digital services taxes [DSTs]) create double taxation of digital suppliers, which are subject to tax both in their residence country and in the market jurisdictions where they operate. New tax claims also pose challenges for revenue recognition, since the new value creation paradigm seems to overlook the fact that value needs to be monetized to generate taxable income, which may occur or not. Other aspects to be considered are the tax impact of legal structures and monetization strategies used to develop digital business models, which leads to an analysis of the applicability of the substance-over-form doctrine and the double revenue threshold mechanism in connection with tax progressivity and tax discrimination effects.

Avoidance of Double Taxation

The digital debate comes down to a clash of national economic interests, where market jurisdictions claim new taxing rights at the expense of eroding the tax bases of other countries where foreign digital suppliers are tax residents. As a result, absent an agreement between conflicting tax claims, double taxation arises, affecting not only digital businesses but also individual customers, who ultimately bear the additional tax burden derived from such double taxation.

Double taxation may exist in two forms: economic and juridical. To begin with, we refer to juridical double taxation, which is defined as the imposition of comparable taxes in two countries on the same taxpayer in respect of the same subject matter for identical periods. Accordingly, the introduction of unilateral measures to tax digital business models without a physical presence in a market jurisdiction creates juridical double taxation on digital suppliers operating outside their countries of residence, if those countries of residence apply a worldwide taxation system. If their countries of residence apply a territorial tax system, which only taxes income earned domestically, then, in principle, no juridical double taxation should arise, since income earned in foreign markets would only be taxed therein by such unilateral tax measures. This issue demands further analysis, which is conducted in chapter 5.

Traditionally, companies have physically provided services in foreign countries without the activities constituting a permanent establishment due to the lack of a fixed place of business (building sites and construction or installation projects for a duration not exceeding the statutory period of time required to create a permanent establishment). Thus, income could be considered local-source income and be subject to withholding tax in the country where services are physically provided and, at the same time, be subject to tax in the country of residence of the company, if a worldwide tax system is applied. To prevent juridical double taxation, tax treaties could provide for an exemption from such withholding tax or a reduced tax rate; in the absence of a tax treaty, the country of residence could provide unilateral tax relief (a tax credit).

Accordingly, if tax-disruptive digital business models that render digital services in market jurisdictions without such activities constituting a permanent establishment were to be subject to an income-based withholding tax therein, a similar solution could be offered to prevent double taxation, since both scenarios are substantially similar. Unfortunately, the majority of initiatives and unilateral tax measures are based on turnover, which falls outside the scope of income tax treaties. Neither measure can be credited against income-based taxes in residence jurisdictions. Therefore, if double taxation is to be avoided, any initiative to tax the digital economy must be based on income, so tax treaty benefits and unilateral tax credits may be applied.

However, taxation of local-source income in the case of companies providing physical services is supported by the benefit principle because, given the physical nature of the services, the government of the market jurisdiction does provide physical infrastructure and a legal environment for the benefit of foreign companies. This is not the case for foreign digital suppliers, which, as already seen, do not derive any benefits from the governments of market jurisdictions where they operate their tax-disruptive digital business models, given the intangible nature of their content. In the absence of a benefit, taxation of local-source income derived from digital suppliers may be difficult to justify on the basis of traditional tax theory, which would ultimately eliminate the issue of double taxation.

A different approach to preventing double taxation would be to establish the obligation for all foreign digital companies wishing to operate in a market jurisdiction to register as permanent establishments or to incorporate as local subsidiaries. If market jurisdictions required this registration as a precondition to operate in their territories, permanent establishment norms would be applicable and double taxation would be addressed by tax treaties or unilaterally by residence countries via tax credits—always on the basis of income. Yet this new scenario, where foreign digital suppliers are compelled to operate through permanent establishments in market jurisdictions, may exacerbate the risk of base erosion (profit shifting to entities subject to no or very low taxation). This risk should be addressed by existing transfer pricing rules rather than by new tax norms outside the scope of the G-20 mandate (Pillar Two of the OECD's Programme of Work).

On a different note, unilateral measures aimed at taxing non-tax-disruptive digital business models create economic double taxation, which can be defined as the taxation imposed on two different persons in respect of the same income or capital. In this case, the persons taxed are the foreign digital supplier and the local entities providing logistical support for its operations, since goods and services are tangible for non-tax-disruptive digital business models. This situation creates not only economic double taxation, but also discrimination in the tax treatment of the domestic and cross-border digital economy. More precisely, digital suppliers that are tax residents or operate through a permanent establishment in the market territory have the right to deduct operating costs (logistics) to assess their taxable income. In contrast, foreign digital suppliers without any physical presence are taxed on their gross revenue according to the new unilateral tax measures (DST), without having the right to be taxed on their real profit after deducting all operating costs.

Consequently, the digital transaction is taxed not only twice, from both the supplier side (direct taxation) and the customer side (indirect taxation), but thrice in the case that certain functions of the digital value chain are outsourced to local providers (storage, distribution, customer care) that are subject to tax as residents in the market jurisdiction. In normal circumstances, as mentioned, the revenue of local providers would be a tax-deductible cost for the suppliers. This is not the case when foreign digital suppliers are subject to tax on their gross revenues. From a tax perspective, the market country taxes the same income stream from a single digital transaction twice. By imposing new revenue-based taxes on foreign digital suppliers, while also taxing local entities providing logistical support for their operations, market jurisdictions are double dipping on the same economic transaction from a direct taxation viewpoint, which creates economic double taxation.

Tax Impact of Legal Structures

The choice of legal structure used to conduct any business does have an impact on the resulting typology of business model and its taxation (legal schemes may be used to avoid permanent establishment status artificially), especially across countries, where different legal and tax systems apply. More precisely, several factors are of utmost importance to determining the type of business model and its tax implications:

- Legal aspects like control over the material means needed to carry out the business activity
- Nature and degree of dependency between the company and the individuals rendering the services
- Characteristics of the chosen monetization strategy
- Use of multiple legal structures in different countries by the same company.

All of these considerations are of exceptional relevance for the digital economy and have particular repercussions on digital and tax-disruptive digital business models.

To begin with, the level of control that a foreign digital supplier exercises over the material means located in the market country needed to carry out the business activity (physical facilities) is relevant to determining whether the foreign digital supplier has a fixed place of business in the market jurisdiction that constitutes a permanent establishment. On the one hand, if the foreign digital company has control over such physical facilities (branch, office, factory, workshop), either as an owner or as a lessee, thereby having the right to use them, it will be deemed to have a permanent establishment in the market territory and be subject to tax therein accordingly. On the other hand, if such physical facilities are under the control of a third party, even if it is a subsidiary of the foreign digital entity, then the foreign digital supplier will not be deemed to have a permanent establishment status in the market jurisdiction. These considerations apply to all digital business models, although non-tax-disruptive digital business models (online sale of tangible goods or services) have a greater need for physical onsite logistics support given their tangible content.

The degree of control over the material means may also have an impact on the type of digital business model. Accordingly, entities with their own physical infrastructure in the market jurisdiction are more likely to operate a digital business model that monetizes through the online sale of tangible goods and services, whereas digital companies with no material means at their disposal may choose to act as brokers and to operate under a tax-disruptive digital business model (online e-commerce marketplace) that monetizes by charging a transactional fee for each trade executed between users of the digital platform. For example, the same online ride-hailing services may be provided through multiple legal structures with very different tax implications:

- By a foreign digital company that owns both the digital platform and the vehicle fleet and hires the drivers (digital business model with a physical presence in the market country)
- By a foreign company that provides the digital platform to connect users who need a ride with private drivers who have their own vehicle (tax-disruptive digital business model without any physical presence)
- By a foreign digital platform operator that charges a transactional fee to a local company that hires drivers and provides them with the material means (a vehicle fleet).

In this last case, if the digital platform operator and the local company were deemed to be related parties for transfer pricing purposes, then transfer pricing issues could arise that would need to be addressed by local transfer pricing laws. As already explained, base erosion and profit-shifting issues should not be used as a pretext to influence taxation of the digital economy and should be dealt with separately.

Another example of the relevance of legal structures is the case of gambling activities, which may be conducted under different business models, depending on whether the user gambles against the digital supplier or against other users of the digital platform. In the first situation, online users place bets (online sports betting) or play games (online slots);

the website operator bears the risk of the gambling outcome, which obviously requires higher financial controls to guarantee the payment of prizes as well as stricter monitoring of the technology used to ensure the fairness of the games (enough online jackpots and prizes are awarded). This monetization strategy is associated with the online gambling tax-disruptive digital business model. However, if users gamble against other users on the digital platform (online poker, online casino), then the platform operator's financial risk is significantly minimized since the monetization strategy shifts to merely a brokerage activity, where the platform charges a transactional fee for each bet placed or takes a percentage commission on the gains from the game. This is a multisided digital platform that operates as an online e-commerce marketplace tax-disruptive digital business model; it acts as a clearinghouse for online gamblers' activities, as a broker connecting gamblers, and also as a gambling platform providing the technology and the virtual space to conduct the gambling and betting activities. As shown, the choice of legal structure has a direct impact on the type of digital business model, on its monetization strategy, on its taxation, and on the functions and risks associated with the digital business activity.

As refers to the degree of dependency of human resources, digital companies may decide to outsource the part of their activity that requires onsite human intervention or may opt to hire employees and build an in-house workforce. Under the first scenario, the human resources act as independent contractors or as employees of a separate legal entity. In principle, this approach eliminates the dependency factor that could give rise to the existence of a dependent agent of the foreign digital supplier in the market jurisdiction and create a permanent establishment therein. For example, in a digital business model where customers' orders are placed and paid for online, physical delivery of the tangible goods may be outsourced to a local entity that provides logistical support services. This approach is economically efficient—it allows flexibility in adapting to the volume of orders to be delivered, without the need to keep a permanent workforce—but it may have an impact on service quality. Under the second scenario, local employees of a foreign digital supplier are deemed to be dependent agents, and, therefore, a permanent establishment exists for tax purposes. However, the same result may be achieved by incorporating a local subsidiary, which would lower the foreign company's tax and legal exposure in the market jurisdiction.

As seen, legal schemes may be devised to prevent permanent establishment status in market jurisdictions, basically by avoiding control over material means and outsourcing human resource needs. In other words, the same business model may be pursued in ways that minimize the taxable presence of a firm in the market country. Moreover, alternative legal structures may prove to be not only tax advantageous, but also economically efficient, since having a greater presence in terms of material means and human resources implies the assumption of higher financial obligations and higher risks for the companies. In the case of foreign digital suppliers, these obligations and risks may prove challenging in the midst of uncertain initiatives to tax their activities in market jurisdictions. Another very important factor to be considered when designing legal structures is, obviously, the legal system and the tax regime applicable in every country, because the same legal structure may have different tax treatments and legal consequences. For this reason, it is not uncommon to find digital companies operating in different countries through different legal structures depending, for example, on labor and administrative regulations (license to operate in certain sectors like ride-hailing services, banking, insurance, or gambling), which result in different digital business models, diverse monetization strategies, and varying tax implications. In cases where legal schemes are aimed at unduly avoiding taxation, countries may apply anti-avoidance measures, like resorting to the substance-over-form doctrine, which would allow tax authorities to disregard the legal structures used and to tax digital business models based on their underlying economic rationale, rather than on artificial legal schemes. This is difficult to do in practice, and even high-income countries struggle to apply this doctrine.

Tax Dimension of Monetization Strategies

The monetization strategies used by digital businesses are interrelated with the type of business model, the legal structure, and the invoicing scheme that determines the direction of the flows of income. For example, multisided digital platforms acting as brokers charge a transactional fee, but they can do that in many different ways, based on the scope of services provided by the platform (channel to connect, payment processing, fulfillment services). Multisided platforms may charge the brokerage fee to only one of the parties or may split it between both parties to the transaction. They can charge a fee in advance to gain access to the database of users of the platform or after the transaction is completed. Moreover, the fee may be charged directly to the parties, it may be deducted from the price of the transaction, or it may be charged to the provider of payment-processing services.

Online suppliers of digital content may monetize in different forms, either through sale, licensing, or subscription models, which may affect the characterization of the proceeds obtained, depending on the legal framework of each market jurisdiction. Similarly, the sale of user data may be treated differently based on the nature and scope of the rights associated with the data being transferred as well as on the value added by the digital company when processing such data. For example, depending on the terms agreed by users and digital businesses that trade with user data and digital content, users may grant rights to access the data for internal use only (technical enhancements, quality control, process improvements) or to process the data and distribute it to third parties for commercial purposes (sale). Similarly, user-targeted advertising may be provided either directly by the same digital company that previously compiled and processed the data or indirectly by third-party online advertising companies that acquire the ad placements (understood as a specific group of ad units on which advertisers can choose to place their ads using placement targeting) to commercialize them to advertisers. The former business model monetizes differently from the latter, since the target customers are totally different, as are the nature and scope of the services provided (advertising versus ad placement).

Obviously, monetization strategies and invoicing schemes have an impact on the tax presence of digital business models in market jurisdictions in connection with the legal structures, as analyzed. For instance, monetization strategies that revolve around the notion of brokerage fees are less prone to be subject to taxation on the basis of taxable presence, since digital platform operators are not parties to the underlying transaction, but rather facilitators. In contrast, digital business models are involved directly in digital transactions as suppliers of digital content for an economic consideration. Furthermore, invoicing schemes must be aligned with digital monetization strategies to avoid conflicting flows of income and, most important, to support the legal structure that determines the roles, duties, and obligations of the parties to the transaction. While this is not specific to digital business models, the risk of incurring contradictory billing mechanisms is exacerbated in the digital economy, which may result in other questionable tax practices, such as transfer pricing, treaty abuse, or tax evasion.

The scope of legal obligations and the extent of the liability of the digital company may be affected by the invoicing scheme since, despite the terms of the legal contract that ultimately governs the digital transaction, customers tend to identify as their contractual counterparty the firm to which they make the payment, irrespective of whether the recipient then settles the associated costs with other providers. Therefore, billing constitutes supporting evidence of the legal appearance of a transaction, which may be used when applying anti-avoidance measures (substance-over-form doctrine). As an example, booking sites (accommodation, travel) may opt to bill only their fee to one or both of the parties, while the parties privately arrange for payment of the service or may choose to collect from the customer the full price with the built-in commission fee and later transfer the payment of the service to the supplier. In this case, the digital platform may incur greater liability, not only financially, but also at a tax level. If a unilateral tax measure is applied in the form of a turnover-based withholding tax, the volume of revenue will determine the tax to be withheld, unless appropriate accounting and financial mechanisms are in place to identify and allocate under separate accounts the different cash flows, always aligned and supported by the terms of the underlying legal contracts.

Accordingly, invoicing arrangements might have significant tax implications if revenue-based taxes were introduced at a general scale to tax the digital economy. They might artificially misrepresent the real volume of business activity of digital business models that opt to retain control over the financial payments. They might do this to limit their risk exposure in case of breach of contract or any other incident attributable to the supplier, which would ultimately result in reimbursement claims, or to secure their liquidity. Initiatives also may include tax thresholds and simplification regimes, whose correct application might be affected by the overreporting of business revenues as well as the tax liability of digital platforms that process third-party payments in their role as withholding agents.

Value Creation versus Revenue Recognition

Newly created tax claims by market jurisdictions pose challenges for revenue recognition since market jurisdictions aim to replace the physical nexus with a new value creation paradigm in which value is created within the market territory by users who contribute data and digital content. Such value must be monetized to generate taxable revenue, which may occur or not, since the mere compilation of data may be worthless without the appropriate technology to process it. Moreover, this raises the question of whether the value lies in the data or in the technology: surely it lies in both, and that is the problem. Therefore, taxation of nonexistent revenue becomes an aggravated tax burden since it is a form of presumptive taxation, based on potential value creation. Digital suppliers also incur an economic cost when they grant free access to digital content in exchange for user data.

The reason why market jurisdictions have resorted to this new paradigm of value creation is that, according to traditional tax theory, in order to apply taxation based on taxable source in the absence of a taxable presence (permanent establishment), it is necessary to demonstrate that the services supplied were effectively rendered in the source country, which is hard to prove for tax-disruptive digital business models. Without physical nexus to the market territory, taxing tax-disruptive digital business models is challenging from the perspective of both taxable source and taxable presence. This challenge leads to the need to replace the traditional nexus with a new value creation paradigm that justifies taxation based on taxable source. Yet replacing one nexus rule by the other implies shifting away from the benefit principle. Previously, local-source taxation was justified on the basis of benefits received from the government of the market jurisdiction by foreign suppliers effectively rendering services in the territory, even if no taxable presence could be established. Under the new value creation paradigm, the value derived by foreign digital suppliers without any physical presence in the territory is no longer connected to the benefits provided by the government; rather, it is connected to the contributions made by the population of users located therein. As already discussed, users usually are compensated by granting them free access to digital content and platforms. Furthermore, even if users are not compensated, they have the right to make any free contribution they wish, without triggering any government right to attract taxation. Otherwise, governments would be claiming rights arising from private actions that are excluded from the public arena and are unrelated and unsupported by public resources. This situation mainly affects user-centered tax-disruptive digital business models, as shown in table 4.1.

Table 4.1 Potential Revenue Recognition Issues of Business Models

Digital and tax-disruptive digital business model	*Potentially taxed ahead of time on nonexistent revenue?*
Digital business models (all types)	X
Tax-disruptive digital business models	
1. Sale of nonuser digital content	X
2. Licensing of nonuser digital content	X
3. Subscription to nonuser digital content	X
4. Virtual banking	X
5. Virtual insurance	X
6. Online gambling	X
7. Online e-commerce marketplace	X
8. Sale of user-related data and digital content	✓
9. Online user-targeted advertising	✓
10. Sale of user-related goodwill	✓

Source: Original table for this publication.

Thus, new unilateral digital taxes may potentially tax user-centered tax-disruptive digital business models on nonexistent revenue presumptively derived from value creation occurring within the market territory. In this respect, we refer to nonexistent revenue rather than to unrealized revenue because, though related, recognition is different from realization. According to the revenue recognition accounting principle, revenues are recognized and earned when they are realized or realizable (usually when services are rendered or goods are transferred), no matter when cash is received. In the context of the new value creation paradigm, no goods or services are involved, just user-related contributions; no realization exists, much less recognition, until the digital company monetizes through the sale of data, goodwill, or advertising services. This situation creates a serious timing issue of revenue recognition, which is not to be confused with issues related to taxation of income accrued, which has been earned but not yet received. It also should not be confused with tax issues related to the taxation of nonexistent income of nonprofitable digital businesses subject to newly introduced turnover-based digital taxes in market jurisdictions. In these two events, there is recognized revenue, unlike in our first case.

Double Revenue Threshold Mechanism

The tax principle of generality is a reflection of the broader characteristic of law that requires tax norms to be applicable to all taxpayers. It does not mean that fiscal benefits and exemptions may not exist. The principle of generality constitutes a specification of the principle of equality, which requires that all taxpayers contribute on the same, equal terms. Therefore, although the principle itself demands impersonality and abstraction, it is not incompatible with personalized tax treatment, as long as the treatment is not arbitrary. To this end, it is mandatory to provide the appropriate motivation to exclude certain taxpayers from general application of the tax norms. In this context, the use of tax thresholds, which some unilateral tax measures incorporate, is controversial.

Tax thresholds may serve different functions. For example, they may segment taxpayers into different tax regimes (simplified tax obligations for smaller businesses, enhanced reporting obligations for specific sectors of activity, tax registration duties by type of business) to facilitate tax compliance and make tax enforcement more efficient, or they may introduce an additional layer of tax progressivity by excluding certain taxpayers from the obligation to pay taxes, similar to an exemption or fiscal benefit. The latter is an expression of the tax principle of vertical equity, which is normally applied to personal income taxation rather than to corporate income taxation, where tax progressivity is uncommon.

In this context, digital services taxes introduced by some market jurisdictions as well as multilateral tax initiatives currently under debate (OECD's Unified Approach under Pillar One) use revenue thresholds as a key element to determine the scope of application of such tax measures. For example, the OECD Secretariat's Proposal for a Unified Approach creates a new nexus based on sales, which could have country-specific sales thresholds that would be used as the primary indicator of a sustained and significant involvement in the market jurisdiction, replacing the traditional nexus that is dependent on physical presence. Additionally, a global revenue threshold could be introduced, as for country-by-country reporting (€750 million).

Enacted DSTs and tentative proposals have also introduced this double revenue threshold: a global revenue threshold (set at €750 million in Austria, the Czech Republic, France, Italy, Spain, and Turkey; £500 million in the United Kingdom; and Can$1 billion in Canada) plus a local revenue threshold (€3 million in Spain and Turkey, €4 million in the Czech Republic, €5 million in Italy, €25 million in Austria and France, £25 million in the United Kingdom, and Can$40 million in Canada). Some proposals have even replaced the local revenue threshold with a regional one (Belgium's failed proposal established a European Union revenue threshold of €50 million), while others only use a single revenue threshold (Ft 100 million in Hungary). Indeed, most unilateral tax measures and proposals have introduced revenue thresholds to limit their scope of application. The double revenue threshold mechanism exempts from taxation all digital companies that do not meet both thresholds. If the company only meets one threshold, it falls outside the scope of taxation, which becomes a powerful tool to exempt local digital companies that are successful only or primarily in the domestic market, but do not reach the highest global revenue threshold set for operations worldwide.

As a result of the significantly higher global revenue threshold, this double revenue threshold system not only introduces tax progressivity, but also de facto discriminates against digital companies with global operations. The use of thresholds is also discriminatory because major local companies operating online marketplaces escape the global revenue threshold only because the covered services still account for a minority of their revenues (sales by third-party sellers are still significantly less than their own direct sales); in contrast, large technology firms that were established as internet companies from the beginning and whose business models were based on delivering the services covered by DSTs are affected and essentially penalized for their commercial success. Furthermore, thresholds are set arbitrarily, and the global revenue threshold has been replicated from the country-by-country reporting requirement (€750 million), which bears no direct relationship with the digital economy. Surely it is intentional that the same threshold used to assess the transfer pricing risks of multinational companies is also used to tax the digital economy. As a result, the threshold exclusively targets multinational digital companies, the majority of which are tax resident in very few specific jurisdictions (China, the United States).

As refers to the tax progressivity effect of revenue thresholds, some observations are required. First, the digital economy is business centered and subject to corporate taxation, where tax progressivity hardly applies. Second, vertical equity, which is the basis for tax progressivity, fulfills an income redistribution function by taxing more heavily those taxpayers with higher incomes, not those with higher revenues. Third, digital business models may easily avoid revenue thresholds by way of fragmenting their operations to fall below them, given their lack of a physical presence. For all of these reasons, the use of tax thresholds in digital economy taxation should be discouraged.

Bibliography

Jaller, Lillyana, Simon Gaillard, and Martín Molinuevo. 2020. *The Regulation of Digital Trade: Key Policies and International Trends*. Washington, DC: World Bank Group.

Klein, Daniel, Christopher Ludwig, and Christoph Spengel. 2019. "Ring-Fencing Digital Corporations: Investor Reaction to the European Commission's Digital Tax Proposals." ZEW Discussion Paper 19-050, Leibniz Centre for European Economic Research, Mannheim University, October.

Lassmann, Andrea, Federica Liberini, Antonio Russo, Ángel Cuevas, and Rubén Cuevas. 2020. "Taxation and Global Spillovers in the Digital Advertising Market: Theory and Evidence from Facebook." CESifo Working Paper 8149, CESifo, Munich.

Mukherjee, Sovik. 2020. "Taxing the Untaxed Digital Economy with a Focus on India: Decoding the Outsourced Holding Company Model." In *Digital Business Strategies in Blockchain Ecosystems,* edited by Umit Hacioglu. Cham: Springer.

Olbert, Marcel, and Christoph Spengel. 2019. "Taxation in the Digital Economy: Recent Policy Developments and the Question of Value Creation." ZEW Discussion Paper 19-010, Leibniz Centre for European Economic Research, Mannheim University.

Richter, Wolfram. 2019a. "Aligning Profit Taxation with Value Creation." CESifo Working Paper 7589, CESifo, Munich.

Richter, Wolfram. 2019b. "The Economics of the Digital Services Tax." CESifo Working Paper 7863, CESifo, Munich.

Ting, Antony, and Sidney Gray. 2019. "The Rise of the Digital Economy: Rethinking the Taxation of Multinational Enterprises." *Journal of International Business Studies* 50 (9): 1656–67.

CHAPTER 5

Tax Policy Issues of Taxing the Digital Economy

This chapter analyzes the impact of the digital economy on the taxing rights of countries from multiple perspectives: source versus residence taxation, worldwide versus territorial taxation, and taxable presence versus taxable source. As a continuation of this discussion, the new nexus rule based on sales, which has been proposed in the Unified Approach of the Organisation for Economic Co-operation and Development (OECD), is explained, critically reviewed, and contrasted with the traditional rule of physical presence. The distinction between routine and residual profits and the revised profit allocation rules are also analyzed, while the use of presumptive tax methods like turnover taxation by digital services taxes (DSTs) is compared to traditional income taxation. Finally, taxation of other types of digital income (capital gains, interests, royalties) is considered.

Digital Impact on Taxing Rights

Countries may exercise taxing rights based on different criteria: connection with individuals or entities, based on having their residence in the territory; connection with the income, based on having its source in the territory; and, even, connection with individuals, based on their having a certain immigration status in the territory, regardless of tax residence (United States citizens and lawful permanent residents living abroad). Only residence and source criteria are applicable to taxation of the digital economy, as analyzed in chapter 3 in connection with the application of traditional tax principles. In this chapter, we move beyond traditional tax theory to evaluate alternative approaches to taxing the digital economy and examine the taxing rights of countries.

The scope of taxing rights of both residence and source countries is analyzed, as applicable to the digital economy. When the taxing rights of both jurisdictions overlap, juridical double taxation arises, as already discussed. It is fundamental to identify clearly the circumstances under which conflicting claims over taxing rights appear and to determine the impact of the digital economy on the traditional allocation of taxing rights between residence and source countries. From the perspective of residence countries, taxing rights vary depending on whether the jurisdiction applies a worldwide taxation system or a territorial taxation system. From the perspective of source countries, taxing rights vary depending on whether the nexus is the taxable source or the taxable presence therein (permanent establishment). As shown in figure 5.1, the allocation of taxing rights under the traditional physical presence nexus rule poses some tax challenges when applied to digital business models.

As shown, when the residence country applies a worldwide taxation system, conflicting taxing rights overlap, and double taxation arises. Such double taxation can only be avoided either by allocating taxing rights under a tax treaty or by providing unilateral relief as a tax credit. Double taxation also may arise when the residence

Figure 5.1 Allocation of Taxing Rights as Applied to Digital Business Models

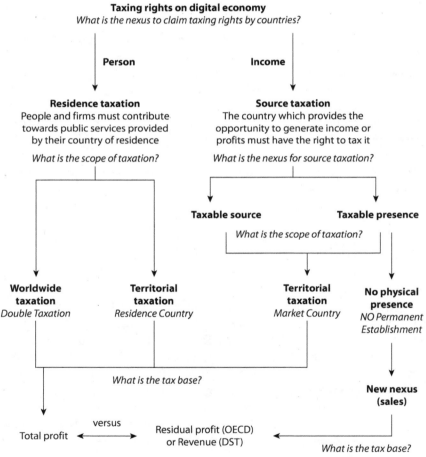

Source: Original figure for this publication.

Note: OECD = Organisation for Economic Co-operation and Development; DST = digital services tax.

country applies territorial taxation and both jurisdictions claim that the digital activity takes place in their territories. However, determining the source of income from digital businesses differs widely based on the physical or intangible nature of the object of the economic transaction. Accordingly, digital business models, which involve the trading of physical goods or commodities and the rendering of physical services, must be differentiated clearly from tax-disruptive digital business models, which are characterized by the supply of intangible digital content.

Regarding digital business models, physical services are taxed differently than physical goods or commodities. Taxing rights on income from physical services are allocated to the jurisdiction where the services are physically performed. For instance, income from services physically rendered abroad without a fixed place of business (building sites and construction or installation projects for a duration not exceeding the statutory period of time required to create a permanent establishment) may be considered local-source income in the foreign country where physical services are provided and may be subject to withholding tax therein. Similarly, income derived by a digital company that renders physical services in a foreign country may be considered local-source income in the market jurisdiction and, therefore, subject to withholding tax on income therein.

Regarding physical goods or commodities, the place where they are bought and sold and where contracts are negotiated and executed, which may be interpreted differently across countries, may have implications when determining the source of income obtained by digital business models from the trade of physical goods or commodities. For instance, income from contracts concluded via electronic means is generally considered local-source income in the country where the digital company operates and is tax resident—that is, the residence jurisdiction. However, the market jurisdiction may also claim taxing rights over the same income on the basis that contracts are executed in its territory and governed by local consumer protection laws or that physical goods or commodities are manufactured or bought and sold therein. Accordingly, several facts have to be assessed when determining the source of income from international trading profits, and each territorial tax jurisdiction has its own set of definitions, interpretations, and jurisprudence. Therefore, each specific digital business model must be analyzed separately, taking into account all of the facts and considerations.

In contrast, tax-disruptive digital business models derive income from digital content, which comprises digital services, digital goods, and access to digital platforms. Given its intangible nature, determining the source of income from digital content poses a double challenge: for the market jurisdiction, to demonstrate that digital activity took place therein, despite the lack of any physical presence in the territory, and for the country where the company is fiscally domiciled, to prove that the digital activity was provided in its territory, so it falls within its territorial taxation system. In this regard, the lack of physical presence renders the traditional nexus inapplicable, which prevents the market country from claiming taxing rights on the basis of taxable presence.

The other option is to claim taxing rights on the basis of taxable source, but, once again, it is necessary to prove that the digital supply activity occurs within the market territory, which is subject to interpretation by the different countries. For example, from a direct taxation perspective, the economic activity that generates the taxable income takes place in the residence jurisdiction, where the digital company has its workforce and technology that make it possible to supply the digital content remotely; from an indirect taxation perspective, which focuses on the consumption side of the digital transaction, the taxable activity takes place in the market jurisdiction, where users and customers are located. In this scenario, where a digital company operates a tax-disruptive digital business model across jurisdictions and is resident in a country that applies territorial taxation, the remote supply of digital content should be deemed to have been conducted locally for a foreign client, and the corresponding fees should be treated as local-source income in the digital company's country of residence. This position is supported by the rule that allocates taxing rights to the residence jurisdiction, when contracts are concluded via electronic means, as is the case for tax-disruptive digital business models.

Figure 5.1 also shows how the physical presence nexus rule could be replaced by a new nexus based on the volume of sales of the digital supplier in the market jurisdiction, as proposed by the OECD's Unified Approach, which is analyzed next. However, although sales are used to establish a taxable presence in the market country, the tax base of this proposal is still income based. In contrast, the tax base of digital services taxes is revenue based, which increases the risk of double taxation, since traditional income-based relief mechanisms are not available to offset turnover-based taxes. At the same time, a double revenue threshold is used to limit the scope of application.

Sales Threshold as a New Nexus Rule

The revision of nexus rules for source taxation can be addressed either from a taxable presence approach, which is the connection between a market jurisdiction and a person deemed to have a physical presence therein (permanent establishment), or from a taxable source perspective, which is the connection between a market jurisdiction and income derived therein. In both cases, nexus rules set the minimum requirements for source countries to impose taxes on income derived by foreign digital companies from operations conducted in the market territory, like in a territorial taxation system.

The taxable presence perspective aims to formulate a new nexus that overcomes the limitation of physical presence and enables taxation of new digital business models that operate either remotely or through a limited local presence and derive income from the market jurisdiction. This is the idea behind the significant economic presence proposal. The taxable source approach aims to establish a new source of taxable income derived from value creation activities happening in the market jurisdiction. This is the rationale behind the user participation and market intangibles proposals, both of which are built into Pillar One. This section focuses only on the new nexus rule based on the significant economic presence proposal.

The significant economic presence proposal was first advocated by the Group of 24 and described in the Base Erosion and Profit Shifting (BEPS) Action 1 Final Report (OECD 2015). The proposal aims to expand the definition of taxable presence. According to the proposal, a taxable presence would arise in a jurisdiction when a nonresident company has a significant economic presence on the basis of a combination of factors, including, but not limited to, revenue generated on a sustained basis, that evidence a purposeful and sustained interaction with the country via technology and other automated means. Apart from the revenue requirement, which is mandatory, other factors include:

- Existence of a user base and the associated data input
- Volume of digital content derived from the jurisdiction
- Billing and collection in local currency or with a local form of payment
- Maintenance of a website in a local language
- Responsibility for the final delivery of goods to customers
- Responsibility for the provision by the company of other support services (after-sales services, repairs, maintenance)
- Sustained marketing and sales promotion activities, online or not, to attract customers.

This initial proposal served as the starting point for developing the new sales-based nexus rule proposed under the OECD's Unified Approach, which significantly expands its original scope (OECD 2019).

The new nexus rule of the OECD's Unified Approach would apply to large consumer-facing businesses that generate revenue from supplying consumer products or providing digital services that have a consumer-facing element. This new rule would define a revenue threshold in the market as the primary indicator of a sustained and significant involvement in the market jurisdiction, irrespective of its level of physical presence in that jurisdiction. Moreover, the revenue threshold would cover certain activities, such as online advertising services, that are directed at nonpaying users in locations that are different from those in which the relevant revenues are booked. However, this scenario could create triple taxation—at the residence jurisdiction, at the source (of the revenues) jurisdiction, and at the country where nonpaying users are located—since the latter could argue that consumer-facing digital services are provided in its territory.

Consequently, the scope of the Unified Approach goes well beyond the scope of the G-20 mandate. It shifts the focus from highly digitalized businesses (what we call tax-disruptive digital business models), which are targeted by the user participation proposal of the United Kingdom, to large consumer-facing businesses, irrespective of their digital nature, which is more aligned with the marketing intangibles proposal first advocated by the United States. The rationale behind this expanded approach is that consumer-facing businesses may use digital technology to develop a consumer base. Nevertheless, the use of digital technology is not required to establish the new nexus, which only uses sales as the primary indicator. Theoretically, the Unified Approach might well apply to traditional business models as well as to digital business models that communicate digitally but trade physical goods and render physical services. Hence, there is no tax-disruptive digital element that requires a new nexus rule based on sales.

The disconnection with the digital scope of the mandate is reflected in the evolution of the factors required to establish the taxable presence. Under the significant economic presence proposal, revenue generated on a sustained basis is the main factor, but not sufficient, since the presence of other factors is required, some of which are linked to the digital activity (volume of digital content derived from the jurisdiction, maintenance of a website in a local language). By contrast, the new sales nexus does not require any additional factors apart from meeting the revenue threshold, which is much broader than the original factor, given that no reference is made to the *sustained basis* of revenue. This intentional omission eliminates the need for business continuity over time. Furthermore, the absence of additional factors linked to the digital activity expands the scope of application to traditional business models, as already mentioned.

Furthermore, according to the Unified Approach, the revenue threshold would create a nexus both for business models involving remote selling to consumers and for groups selling in a market through a distributor (whether a related or nonrelated local entity) to capture all forms of remote involvement in the economy of a market jurisdiction. Baseline distribution and marketing activities, irrespective of their digital nature, would be subject to new profit allocation rules (fixed returns under Amount B) that aim to reduce the dissatisfaction with the current transfer pricing rules. This work is clearly outside the scope of the G-20 mandate. Once again, under the false pretense of addressing the tax challenges of the digital economy, nondigital issues (transfer pricing, dispute resolution, profit shifting) are modified without the appropriate authority.

Another very important criticism of this new sales-based nexus rule is the lack of a real nexus. The proposal uses the revenue threshold as the primary and only indicator of a taxable presence in the market jurisdiction, while the function of tax thresholds has traditionally been to limit the scope of application of tax norms, not to establish a nexus between a taxing jurisdiction and a taxpayer. Indeed, if the volume of sales of a foreign company in a market country suffices to create a taxable presence, then, according to the tax principle of horizontal equity, all traditional business models that are equivalent to digital business models (international trade of physical goods or commodities) and conduct cross-border operations should be taxed in all of those countries where their sales exceed the revenue threshold. Such taxation would contravene the benefit principle and would again exceed the digital scope set by the G-20 mandate. Moreover, the revenue threshold may fulfill a double function as both nexus and tax threshold, which is difficult to reconcile with tax theory since the result would be discriminatory in terms of vertical equity, as discussed in chapter 4, but, in this case, in terms of the nexus.

Additionally, the use of a revenue threshold as nexus would be more consistent with traditional tax theory if applied to establish a taxable source, rather than a taxable presence, since the connection is between the market jurisdiction and the sales therein, not between the market and the foreign supplier. This distinction is relevant because the significant economic presence proposal would assign taxing rights based on taxable presence, which applies to the entire profit of the entity. However, both the user participation and the marketing intangibles proposals would assign taxing rights on taxable source and would only tax residual profit of the entire group. Therefore, the Unified Approach uses a nexus that creates a taxable presence, but the new taxing right (Amount A) applies profit attribution rules more aligned with a taxable source approach (residual profit).

Routine versus Residual Profits

Profit allocation rules determine which and how much profit and losses to attribute for tax purposes in relation to new taxing rights. More specifically, profit allocation rules comprise the scope of profit subject to the new taxing right (all profit or only residual profit, profit from the multinational group, only profit from one or some entities), the choice of method for calculating and allocating profit subject to the new taxing right (residual profit split method, fractional apportionment method), and the preferred treatment of losses (symmetric or asymmetric treatment of profit and losses, use of claw-back or "earn out" mechanism). In short, both the user participation and the marketing intangibles proposals aim to tax residual profit of the multinational group, using the residual profit split method, while the significant economic presence proposal aims to tax all profit, both routine and residual, of the entity operating in the market territory, using the fractional apportionment method, which requires determining the allocation keys and the respective weights for dividing the tax base (sales, assets, employees). The Unified Approach combines both approaches, which poses some tax challenges.

The distinction between routine and residual profits comes from the arm's length principle and its interpretation through the transfer pricing guidelines. On the one hand, routine profit arises from readily identifiable—and generally less complex—business activities for which comparable pricing is available. Under current transfer pricing rules, routine activities are allocated a return benchmarked by reference to reliable comparables. Examples of routine profit are income attributable to technology-related intangibles generated by research and development and income attributable to routine marketing and distribution functions, which is now covered by Amount B. On the other hand, residual profit (also referred to as nonroutine profit) is the profit remaining after routine profit is subtracted from total profit; it is typically allocated to entrepreneurial activities performed within a multinational group. In businesses that are heavily reliant on intangibles, it is generally assumed that residual profit is highly correlated with the return on intangible assets. Calculating residual profit is complex and burdensome given the lack of reliable comparables. Some examples of residual profit are income attributable to ownership of valuable intangibles (marketing related), income from performance of economically significant functions, and income derived from control and assumption of economically significant risks.

Another important difference is the kind of nexus for source taxation associated with each type of profit, since the amount of taxable profit varies depending on whether the taxing right is based on taxable presence or on taxable source. As explained, the user participation and marketing intangibles proposals establish a taxable source that would tax residual profit of the entire multinational group, not only that of the entity operating in the market jurisdiction. The rationale behind this profit allocation is that routine functions, which are linked intrinsically to the core business activity of any company, cannot be conducted in the source country absent a taxable presence; therefore, routine profit cannot be taxed therein. Consequently, taxable source founded on market proposals would only allow market countries to claim taxing rights on residual profit, and such tax claim would extend to the entire multinational group on the basis that economically significant intangibles, functions, and risks are mobile and easy to relocate within a group of entities. This proposal is based on transfer pricing. In contrast, taxable presence established under the significant economic presence proposal would tax all profit, including both routine and residual profits, but only of the entity deemed virtually present in the market jurisdiction. This proposal is more aligned with the traditional taxation of nonresident entities with a taxable presence in a source country.

However, Amount A of the OECD's Unified Approach introduces a new taxing right for market jurisdictions over a portion of a multinational group's deemed residual profit that is within the scope of definition. It combines features of both the residual profit split method, by introducing a threshold based on profitability to exclude the remuneration of routine activities, and the fractional apportionment method, by relying on formula-based calculations. This mixed approach creates some issues due to the conflicting rationales behind the combined methods, as just explained, in connection with the type of nexus. To begin with, the application of a transfer pricing framework (residual profit split method) to the digital economy is not appropriate. Transfer pricing aims to prevent base erosion of residence jurisdictions' taxing rights, while the Unified Approach aims to do the opposite with the same tools—that is, it aims to erode residence jurisdictions' taxing rights in favor of creating new taxing rights, absent a taxable presence that may justify such profit shifting from residence to market countries. Furthermore, residence jurisdictions have taxing rights over all profit of all companies fiscally domiciled therein, which includes both routine and residual profits. For that reason, transfer pricing rules can effectively claim not only routine but also residual profits when multinational groups try to shift residual profit abroad. The Unified Approach does the opposite: it tries to strip away from residence jurisdictions taxing rights over residual profits that are, indeed, protected by transfer pricing rules. Basically, it would require residence jurisdictions to give up taxing rights over income generated by nonroutine business activity.

Another troubling issue about the Unified Approach and the new taxing right under Amount A is the fact that the sales variable is assigned a triple function within the proposed system:

- First, as a primary and only indicator for the new nexus rule, as already discussed
- Second, as a tax threshold that limits the scope of application of the new taxing right, in the form of a country-specific revenue threshold, as also analyzed

- Third, as a key to allocate the relevant portion of the deemed nonroutine profit among the eligible market jurisdictions.

Consequently, the system is sales centered, which poses serious concerns by creating a new direct taxing right on the basis of a consumption variable like revenues from sales. Conversely, it is the same as imposing a new consumption tax based on the physical presence of suppliers in the market jurisdiction, irrespective of whether such suppliers conduct sales or not in the territory. Moreover, digital consumption is already addressed by indirect taxes (value added tax [VAT]/goods and services tax [GST]) and could be taxed further if the World Trade Organization decides to lift the ban on tariffs for digital trade that has been in place since 1998. Therefore, if the aim of the market jurisdiction is to increase tax collections from the digital economy, using customs duties on digital goods may be a better option than introducing new direct tax measures based on sales.

Finally, as pointed out in chapter 3, the real issue about the treatment of tax losses is the loss-absorbing capacity of residence jurisdictions when a digital company goes out of business without having declared any profit, but its tax losses are offset against the profits of other entities in the group, in application of either a tax consolidation regime (Australia, France, Spain, United States) or a system of group relief (United Kingdom). Accordingly, residence countries have to endure the tax sacrifice from failed digital businesses, without sharing it with market jurisdictions. Besides, characterizing profit as routine or residual depends on the type of function, asset, or risk to which the income is attributable, which raises the question of whether tax losses arise only from routine activities or also from entrepreneurial activities that generate residual profit. The answer is that tax losses should also be characterized as routine or nonroutine, depending on the type of activity and the nature of the assets, functions, and risks from which they originate. Market jurisdictions should be allocated and bear tax losses from nonroutine activities, so as to guarantee the symmetric allocation of both residual profits and losses, and loss-making multinational groups should be able to claim tax refunds from market jurisdictions for nonroutine losses.

Income versus Turnover Taxation

This section deals with sales as the tax base, not as nexus, threshold, or allocation key; in other words, it analyzes turnover taxation as applied to the digital economy. This revenue-based tax regime is the core of DSTs that many countries worldwide are increasingly introducing unilaterally. As an alternative to income taxation, turnover taxation is considered a form of presumptive taxation, which consists of inferring the base of taxation from some simple indicators (gross turnover, net assets, net worth) that are easier to measure than going through the regular process of computing income. Presumptive taxation is used mostly as a proxy for income taxation. From a practical perspective, the major issue raised by turnover taxation is the trade-off between accuracy and administrative feasibility. The issue is the extent to which the benefit from improving administrative feasibility of a tax is worth the cost of lowering its accuracy. Another related issue is whether turnover taxation by DSTs should (a) be used as a permanent replacement for income taxation or (b) be viewed as merely a transitional phase until tax administrations are capable of applying income taxation without using presumptions.

Many countries have used turnover taxation as a form of presumptive taxation for decades, but in very different circumstances and for very different reasons. Low- and middle-income countries have used turnover taxation mainly for small businesses—in some cases, as a minimum tax, due to the lack and low reliability of available tax information and the limited tax capacity of tax administrations. Instead, high-income countries apply DSTs to tax digital multinational companies, despite the availability of financial information and the high tax capacity of governments. Some low- and middle-income countries using turnover taxation provide presumptive deductions based on ratios developed for types of industry or income, to acknowledge that different industries have different profit rates. However, DSTs treat all digital business models as if they share similar profit margins, which is far from being true, since cost structures vary widely between tax-disruptive digital business models. Turnover taxation has always been used by residence jurisdictions, while in the current situation this form of presumptive taxation is being enforced by source countries on the basis of dubious tax claims. Traditionally, turnover has been the most easily measured financial variable for a business and is readily available to tax administrations since it must be computed for the payment of other taxes (for example, VAT). The disadvantage of a turnover-based tax is that turnover bears no necessary relationship to any measure of income, so it does not provide a good proxy for income.

Consequently, it is difficult to see the attractiveness of turnover taxation beyond the fact that it is relatively easy to administer and thus raises revenue. Given that most of the jurisdictions that have introduced DSTs are high-income countries with robust tax administrations, the only plausible reason for the choice of revenue as a tax base is the deliberate intent to prevent any conflict in the application of tax treaties and other income-based tax regulations in force. Therefore, from a policy perspective, the most interesting issue is to determine the extent to which presumptions like turnover taxation can be used to simplify the task of tax administrations without fundamentally changing the tax base, as happens with DSTs.

Furthermore, presumptive techniques have traditionally been employed for a variety of reasons, including, but not limited to, combatting tax avoidance and tax evasion; simplifying and reducing the burden of tax compliance for taxpayers with very low turnover; achieving a more equitable distribution of the tax burden by providing objective indicators for tax assessment to limit administrative corruption; or promoting and encouraging taxpayers to keep proper books and records on the basis of which their actual income may be properly taxed. None of these reasons is applicable to digital services taxes.

High-income countries have an income tax structure that has evolved over the last two centuries away from presumption, which led most of them to reject revenue-based taxation in the 1960s. Therefore, it is surprising that, in the 21st century, the same high-income countries, which have much greater tax administration capacity, are resorting to an outdated form of taxation to claim their share of the digital economy. Historically, presumptive taxes offered a way for low- and middle-income countries to achieve a substantive broadening of the tax base, given their economic structure and the information vacuum in which their tax administrations were forced to function. This scenario is the opposite of the current use of turnover-based DSTs. Indeed, experience suggests that the shortcomings of presumptive taxation stem mostly from a lack of clear objectives. When overstretched for revenue purposes, a presumptive tax may lead to corruption and oppression of taxpayers, even for digital multinationals. Furthermore, turnover taxation does not account for costs, which may result in taxation of nonexistent income or profit, creating double taxation that cannot be avoided given that tax treaties are income based and residence jurisdictions do not provide unilateral tax relief for foreign revenue–based taxes. In sum, turnover taxation is inconsistent with prevailing tax principles, with tax administration capacity, and with the digital economy.

Other Types of Digital Income

To begin with, not all tax-disruptive digital business models fall within the scope of either unilateral tax measures or the Unified Approach. None of these initiatives address capital gains from the indirect sale of user-related goodwill and know-how arising from the sale (exit strategy) of digital businesses whose value is enhanced by user-related data, content, and experiences. Moreover, some of these digital companies did not monetize previously in any other way, since their main purpose was to build a user base that would help them to improve the user experience, acquire a better understanding of the business model, and build a comparative advantage that would position them as leaders in the digital market. Therefore, no tax measure is currently targeting capital gains from the indirect sale of user-related activity occurring in a market jurisdiction, which is consistent with traditional tax principles. Any tax claim over such income would be very difficult to justify, as well as to enforce, since, unlike profits, capital gains cannot be categorized as routine or residual, especially without previous monetization. Some famous examples include the sale of YouTube, Waze, or Fitbit to Google; the acquisition of Instagram and WhatsApp by Facebook; and the purchase of LinkedIn and Skype by Microsoft.

Other tax-disruptive digital business models that are not within the scope of unilateral tax measures and tax proposals are virtual banking and virtual insurance. Indeed, the Unified Approach carves out financial services, which go beyond banking and insurance to include credit card companies, consumer-finance companies, stock brokerages, and investment funds, among others. Similarly, no specific tax claims by market jurisdictions are made to tax foreign digital companies in the business of online gambling. All of these business models have in common that their activities are regulated by governments, and it is usually mandatory to obtain a license before legally operating in the jurisdiction, which often implies incorporating a local subsidiary that is taxed as a resident taxpayer. Thus, there is no need for creative tax claims on the basis of new and revised nexus and profit allocation rules.

Nevertheless, it is necessary to differentiate between tax-disruptive digital business models conducted by digital companies and digital transactions involving users who derive income from participating in such business models. For instance, crowdfunding platforms help to raise small amounts of money online from a large number of users, who can provide funds either as debt or as equity, assuming that the projects or ventures are successful and will provide users of online financial or investment activities with interest or dividends. Similarly, users may contribute intellectual property (designs, music, videos, webinars, blogs) to digital content platforms in exchange for royalties paid for distribution or reproduction rights (YouTubers, e-learning, bloggers, influencers), or digital nomads may be hired online through crowdsourcing platforms to perform digital freelance projects without any fixed place of work. Consequently, tax-disruptive digital business models generate not only business income for foreign digital companies but also other types of income (interests, dividends, royalties, remuneration) for users, who are taxed as resident taxpayers in the market country, unless their location of residence is unknown (for example, digital nomads).

Another important issue raised by the different types of digital income received by users is their tax regime when both users are tax residents in different jurisdictions. In that case, both the increase and decrease in income have asymmetrical effects on the countries, and it is not clear where the underlying digital transaction is deemed to take place. For instance, donations made by donors and received by donees through funding websites or platforms, when both are located in different countries, pose a challenge since the residence country of the donor may not provide a tax deduction or the donee's residence country may not provide a tax exemption or some other tax relief. Another example is the case of users who bet against each other (for example, online poker) through an online betting platform that acts as a broker: the gains of one player are the losses of another, and, likewise, the taxable gains in one jurisdiction become losses to offset in the other jurisdiction. Some websites grant users free-of-charge access to online content and digital platforms, which could be deemed taxable compensation in kind in exchange for data. Digital business models that sell physical goods or render physical services in the market jurisdiction are forced to employ a local workforce and usually incorporate a local subsidiary for this purpose (Amazon), since the digital company is responsible for distribution (delivery of physical goods). However, some other businesses only act as brokers (online e-commerce marketplaces) by connecting users (Airbnb, Uber), which may raise tax compliance and enforcement issues.

Therefore, the cross-border nature of digital transactions has a tax impact not only on market jurisdictions regarding foreign digital companies operating in their territories without any physical presence but also on other types of digital income obtained by users across countries. From a policy perspective, users may be taxed on consumption (purchase of digital content), but they may also be taxed on income. The real tax challenge is to enforce taxation on the digital economy.

Bibliography

Aslam, Aqib, and Alpa Shah. 2020. "Tec(h)tonic Shifts: Taxing the 'Digital Economy.'" IMF Working Paper WP/20/76, International Monetary Fund, Washington, DC.

Avi-Yonah, Reuven. 1997. *Presumptive Income Taxation: Proceedings of a Seminar Held in New Delhi in 1997 during the 51st Congress of the International Fiscal Association*, vol. 22. Alphen aan den Rijn: Kluwer Law International.

Avi-Yonah, Reuven. 2018. "Designing a 21st Century Taxing Threshold: Some International Implications of *South Dakota* vs. *Wayfair*." Research Paper 611, University of Michigan, Ann Arbor, June 25, 2018.

Avi-Yonah, Reuven. 2020. "Taxation for a New 'New Deal': Short-, Medium-, and Long-Term Options." University of Michigan, Ann Arbor, May 17, 2020.

Bird, Richard. 2002. "Why Tax Corporations?" *Bulletin for International Fiscal Documentation* 56 (5): 194–203.

Bird, Richard. 2012." Taxation and Development: What Have We Learned from Fifty Years of Research?" International Center for Public Policy Working Paper, Andrew Young School of Policy Studies, Georgia State University, Atlanta.

Bird, Richard, and Jack Mintz. 2020. "International Tax Sharing: Can the Dream Become Reality?" In *The Allocation of Multinational Business Income: Reassessing the Formulary Apportionment Option*, vol. 76, edited by Richard Krever and François Vaillancourt, 299–321. Alphen aan den Rijn: Kluwer Law International.

Bird, Richard, and Oliver Oldman. 1977. "The Transition to a Global Income Tax: A Comparative Analysis." In *Bulletin for International Fiscal Documentation*, 439–54. Amsterdam: International Bureau of Fiscal Documentation.

Bird, Richard, and Scott Wilkie. 2000. "Source vs. Residence Taxation in the European Union: The Wrong Question?" In *Taxing Capital Income in the European Union*, edited by Sijbren Cnossen, 78–109. Oxford: Oxford University Press.

Carpentieri, Loredana, Stefano Micossi, and Paola Parascandolo. 2019. "Overhauling Corporate Taxation in the Digital Economy." *CEPS Policy Insights,* no. 2019-15 (October): 1–19.

Cui, Wei. 2019. "The Superiority of the Digital Services Tax over Significant Digital Presence Proposals." *National Tax Journal* 72 (4): 839–56.

Hamdan, Mohammad Abdul-Jalil. 2019. "Electronic Permanent Establishment: An Option for International Taxation on Profits of Cross-Border Business Transactions in the Context of Digital Economy." *Advances in Social Sciences Research Journal* 6 (10): 63–85.

Hellerstein, Walter, Jeffrey Owens, and Christina Dimitropoulou. 2019. "Digital Taxation Lessons from Wayfair and the U.S. States' Responses." *Tax Notes International* 94: 241.

IMF (International Monetary Fund). 2019. "Corporate Taxation in the Global Economy." IMF Policy Paper 57, International Monetary Fund, Washington, DC.

Kostic, Svetislav. 2019. "In Search of the Digital Nomad: Rethinking the Taxation of Employment Income under Tax Treaties." *World Tax Journal* 11 (2): 189–225.

Krever, Richard, and Peter Mellor. 2020. "History and Theory of Formulary Apportionment." In *The Allocation of Multinational Business Income: Reassessing the Formulary Apportionment Option*, vol. 76, edited by Richard Krever and François Vaillancourt, 9–39. Alphen aan den Rijn: Kluwer Law International.

OECD (Organisation for Economic Co-operation and Development). 2015. *Addressing the Tax Challenges of the Digital Economy, Action 1—2015 Final Report.* OECD/G-20 Base Erosion and Profit Shifting Project. Paris: OECD.

OECD (Organisation for Economic Co-operation and Development). 2019. "Secretariat Proposal for a 'Unified Approach' under Pillar One." Public consultation document, OECD Secretariat, Paris, October 9–November 12, 2019.

OECD (Organisation for Economic Co-operation and Development). 2020. "Tax Challenges Arising from Digitalisation—Report on Pillar One Blueprint: Inclusive Framework on BEPS." OECD/G-20 Base Erosion and Profit Shifting Project, OECD Publishing, Paris.

Rahman, Haseena. 2020. "A Proposal for a Digital Permanent Establishment in Afghanistan." *Tax Notes International* 98 (8): 931–37.

Vella, John. 2019. "Digital Services Taxes: Principle as a Double-Edged Sword." *National Tax Journal* 72 (4): 821–38.

Watson, Garrett. 2019. *Resisting the Allure of Gross Receipts Taxes: An Assessment of Their Costs and Consequences.* Washington, DC: Tax Foundation.

CHAPTER 6

Tax Administration Issues of Taxing the Digital Economy

The real challenge of taxing the digital economy lies not so much in designing taxes as in overcoming tax administration constraints, such as ensuring the tax registration of digital companies without a physical presence in the market jurisdiction, determining the accrual and assessment of taxes for tax-disruptive digital business models, applying the most effective collection method in the absence of a taxable presence, defining the nature of the presumptions on the basis of limited access to information, and enhancing monitoring and enforcement mechanisms to control and tax the digital activity occurring within the country. This chapter discusses all of these tax administration issues, focusing on the direct taxation of foreign digital companies conducting cross-border activities in market jurisdictions. Many of the aspects analyzed are also applicable to digital companies operating within their domestic jurisdiction.

Tax Registration of Foreign Digital Companies

Tax registration is the first stage in tax administration. It allows the tax administration to build a taxpayer base that may help to identify and locate taxpayers, monitor their taxable activity, audit tax compliance, enforce collection and other tax measures, and forecast tax revenues. Overall, tax registration helps to establish a preliminary scope of taxpayers who choose to comply voluntarily with their formal tax obligations and who may be subject to taxation. Tax registration has a central role to play in the administration of taxing rights arising from residence taxation: all persons domiciled in the taxing jurisdiction are subject to tax, constituting the primary source of tax revenues for the country. An additional advantage of resident taxpayers is their physical presence in the territory, which facilitates the enforcement of tax obligations and sanctions in the event of tax offenses. This does not imply that tax registration is not relevant for the taxation of nonresidents—quite the opposite—but it is more challenging, especially in the absence of any physical presence of the taxpayer or its business, as occurs with digital activities.

In this regard, the difficulties of getting nonresident entities to register for tax purposes are widely recognized, as happens with the registration of nonresident digital suppliers for value added tax (VAT)/goods and services tax (GST) purposes, which in some countries extend to nonresident tax agents (digital platforms). Nonresident entities may opt not to register for many reasons, including tax evasion, burdensome registration procedures resulting in complex and non-cost-effective compliance, or simply lack of awareness of the legal requirements and regulations in the market jurisdiction. Regardless of the difficulties, monitoring activities are more challenging without voluntary tax registration. This is especially true for tax-disruptive digital business models, which are intangible in nature and may operate without any external sign of business activity in the market territory.

At this point, and with our focus on direct taxation of foreign digital entities conducting cross-border activities in market jurisdictions, the relevant issue is the extent to which tax registration is necessary and on what premise tax registration could be waived or replaced by other mechanisms that would fulfill a similar function. In this respect, tax registration is the mechanism for establishing communication between a person and a tax administration; such communication may be necessary to comply with tax obligations, which can go beyond paying taxes (submitting tax-relevant information, withholding tax amounts, depositing amounts withheld, monitoring compliance of third parties' tax obligations). In addition to taxpayers, tax agents and tax representatives may also be required to register for tax purposes. Having said that, tax obligations of nonresidents may vary widely, from paying taxes to reporting transactions or withholding amounts, all of which depend on the nexus for establishing the taxing right of the source country. For example, nonresidents who are liable based on taxable presence (permanent establishment) are required to register because their tax liability arises from their physical presence and usually pertains to all income from activity conducted within the territory.

Taxing rights on digital business income would be based on taxable source, which would allow taxing source income via withholdings that would be applied by resident companies or local financial institutions (banks, credit card companies) or by nonresident tax agents (digital platforms), irrespective of whether the foreign digital company is registered or not. Such withholdings would be final, unless nonresident taxpayers were allowed to register and claim refunds on any excess income withheld, subject to submitting a tax return and all supporting documentation (for income-based initiatives, like the Unified Approach of the Organisation for Economic Co-operation and Development [OECD]) or, alternatively, if foreign digital companies were allowed to rebut the presumption on which turnover taxation is based (for digital services taxes [DSTs]). Another option would be to introduce a new presumptive tax on the use of digital data transmission bandwidth collected via withholding by internet service providers (ISPs), as is discussed in chapter 7. Given the extremely high thresholds of current tax measures and proposals, tax registration of foreign digital companies within scope should not be an issue for direct taxation purposes. Instead, if tax thresholds were removed, tax registration could be optional for entities conducting exclusively business-to-business (B2B) transactions and mandatory for entities exceeding a business-to-consumer (B2C) threshold.

Accordingly, tax registration is less relevant both for direct taxation purposes and for nonresident taxpayers, which combined is the exact case of foreign digital companies. While tax registration is important for indirect taxation of B2C transactions where nonresident digital suppliers act as withholding agents of the indirect tax, the situation is the opposite for direct taxation, since nonresident digital suppliers are not withholding agents, but taxpayers. Tax registration also plays a different role for resident taxpayers than for nonresident taxpayers. Resident taxpayers have a physical presence in the country, and tax authorities use tax registration information for enforcement purposes (tax litigation, seizure of property, lien on assets, bank account freeze). In contrast, any enforcement measures adopted against nonresident digital companies without a physical presence in the market jurisdiction are most likely to prove ineffective. As a consequence, the role that tax registration plays for foreign digital companies is limited to mere communication, since, even if registered, nonresident entities may choose not to comply with their tax obligations in the market country, without real consequences. For this reason, in the absence of a taxable presence, source taxation has traditionally been imposed via withholding, and tax registration has not usually been required.

Another option is to introduce a simplified tax registration procedure for foreign digital companies that would provide some type of tax benefits or tax incentives, like expediting refund claims on tax amounts withheld by resident tax agents (private businesses, financial institutions, public entities) that exceed the tax liability or simply are not subject to taxation as a result of not exceeding the taxable threshold (one-time transactions, low-volume B2C businesses) or being exempt. This alternative would be especially relevant for nonresident digital platforms that intermediate in peer-to-peer (P2P) digital transactions (online marketplaces like eBay, Airbnb, online poker sites) and offer payment-processing services, which would result in high amounts withheld, many of which would probably by exempt and have to be refunded by the tax authorities of market jurisdictions, upon simplified reporting obligations.

Therefore, if nonresident digital suppliers were subject to direct taxation in market jurisdictions, tax registration would not be significantly relevant either for compliance or for enforcement purposes; the real challenge would be to secure the collection of taxes at the source, before payments leave the country. To this end, financial entities should act as tax agents and apply withholding on outbound transfers from B2C digital transactions. Unfortunately, the financial sector is not supportive in this respect. Hence, the role that tax registration plays in this context is clearly not central to tax compliance.

Assessment and Accrual of Digital Taxes

This section analyzes assessment and accrual aspects of digital taxes and initiatives, including the link between different tax bases and possible assessment methods as well as the impact of source taxation nexus on the timing of tax accrual, which is also connected to collection mechanisms. Collection mechanisms are addressed in the following section. As already discussed, according to traditional tax principles, market jurisdictions have no basis for claiming taxing rights on income from foreign digital companies, neither on taxable presence, given the lack of a physical presence of nonresident digital suppliers, nor on taxable source, since digital activity neither takes place within the territory nor obtains any benefits from its government. For the sake of discussion, we examine the impact of nexus rules on the timing of accrual of unilateral measures and initiatives to tax the digital economy (DSTs, Unified Approach).

In this regard, we have established that the new nexus based on sales bears a closer correlation with taxable source than with taxable presence. This correlation is relevant because, usually, taxable presence results in periodic accrual of the tax, with the fiscal year being the most common accrual period (permanent establishments are taxed on their yearly income). The accrual period is independent of the timing of tax collection, which may require partial payments on account of the final tax liability or even automatic application of tax withholding on account, to secure liquidity for the government throughout the year. In contrast, taxable source normally results in instantaneous tax accrual, which is reflected in the common tax withholding mechanism applicable to outbound payments made to nonresidents, mostly passive income. It may also affect active income from business activities conducted within the country without a fixed place of business, as analyzed in chapter 5. In this case, tax accrual is transaction based, and tax collection is designed to secure payment irrespective of voluntary tax compliance, since nonresident taxpayers do not play any active role in the process.

However, it is very important to distinguish between source taxation of different types of income based on the need for further computation to assess the tax. Certain types of passive income (dividends, interests, royalties) may be subject to a final withholding tax without additional calculation, while other types of passive income (capital gains, rental income) may require subtracting acquisition costs or maintenance costs to assess the final tax, which may differ from the amount of tax initially withheld. The latter is also the case for source taxation of active income (income from building sites and construction or installation projects for a duration not exceeding the statutory time period required to create a permanent establishment). Under the new sales nexus, source taxation would be applicable to active income from business activities conducted by nonresident digital companies in market jurisdictions without any physical presence. In this scenario, unless turnover taxation is deemed final and the tax presumption is nonrebuttable (DSTs), to assess the final income tax liability, the initial amount of tax withheld on the basis of revenue would be adjusted by subtracting all operating costs from the business activity. Alternatively, to assess the final income tax under Amount A of the Unified Approach, routine profit would be subtracted and a share of residual profit would be allocated to the market country based on local sales, which would result in either additional tax payments or refunds.

A different approach could involve amending turnover-based taxes to allow taxpayers to compute their taxable income according to tax regulations applicable to permanent establishments; all foreign digital companies would be given the opportunity to register a taxable presence in market jurisdictions. This option would solve any tax discrimination issues between foreign suppliers with a taxable presence and digital suppliers without a physical presence. It also would encourage foreign digital companies to incorporate local subsidiaries or to establish branches in the market countries, solving the troublesome lack of a physical presence. This alternative system would rely on rebuttable presumptions, as opposed to current digital services taxes, which do not allow companies to refute the turnover tax.

It is very important to understand the rationale and implications behind the use of rebuttable presumptions, especially in the context of digital economy taxation, where access to the financial and tax information of foreign digital companies is extremely limited. Such a constraint is due to the lack of applicable exchange of information mechanisms, since most instruments like tax treaties and tax information exchange agreements are only applicable in connection with income-based taxes, while current unilateral taxes (DSTs) are revenue based and fall outside the scope of application. Indeed, this is the exact same reason why those taxes are assessed on turnover: to avoid any overlap or conflict with the network of income tax treaties. However, the use of rebuttable presumptions, also known in legal terminology as *iuris tantum* presumptions, provides an opportunity for taxpayers to provide voluntarily the information needed to assess their tax liability and claim any refund that may be due. In contrast, irrebuttable presumptions, also known as *iuris et de iure*, have traditionally been used either as minimum taxes or as exclusive taxes, as discussed next.

Application of Presumptive Digital Taxes

Not only digital services taxes but also Amounts A and B under the Unified Approach are based on presumptions (formulaic approaches, allocation keys, fixed percentages) that, in the event they are finally implemented, could be applied in many different ways. These differences would depend on whether such tax presumptions are rebuttable or not and whether they are mandatory, optional, or merely a safe harbor, as proposed by the United States. Several options for applying such presumptions are available under traditional tax theory and international tax practice and should be considered, such as minimum taxes, exclusive taxes, alternative taxes, or optional taxes. Furthermore, presumptive taxes may be determined collectively or individually. Depending on the degree of discretion allowed to tax officials in the application of presumptive methods, the determination can be mechanical or discretionary, which may affect the flexibility for negotiation.

At a domestic level, irrebuttable presumptions provide neutrality in terms of application, since both tax administrations and taxpayers must accept the resulting legal assessment of the tax liability, without any possibility for making unilateral changes. In contrast, rebuttable presumptions favor the dominant position of tax administrations by shifting the burden of proof to taxpayers, who need to provide supporting evidence of the real tax liability. As a consequence, in the context of domestic taxation, the use of rebuttable presumptions is discouraged, since it is assumed that tax administrations have sufficient information on which to make a tax assessment based on real activity without pushing the burden to taxpayers. However, the situation is the opposite in a cross-border scenario, where market jurisdictions may face great difficulties obtaining information from the countries where digital companies operating in their territories are tax resident. Indeed, rebuttable presumptive assessments have traditionally been used as a means of ascertaining taxpayers' income in the face of inadequate data (when taxpayers either do not fully disclose their financial situations on their returns or fail to file a return). This is the same situation experienced by market jurisdictions when trying to tax foreign digital companies. Accordingly, in an international taxation environment, the use of rebuttable presumptions is recommended over the use of irrebuttable ones. Unfortunately, current tax measures and initiatives to tax the digital economy apply irrebuttable presumptions that prevent taxpayers from proving that their actual income, calculated under tax accounting rules, is less than their income calculated under the presumptive method, which should be revised in light of the circumstances.

As mentioned, irrebuttable presumptions can be divided into two types: minimum taxes, where tax liability is no less than the liability determined according to the presumptive rules, and exclusive taxes, where tax liability is assessed under the presumption alone, even if the regular rules might lead to higher liability. If taxpayers are not given the right to claim a refund, then the withholding tax is in effect a minimum tax collected via withholding. This would be the case for both DSTs and Amounts A and B of the Unified Approach, which also share traits with exclusive taxes, since their tax liabilities are determined under presumption alone. Yet neither is a pure minimum tax, which would be the second-best option—after the use of rebuttable presumptions—for taxing foreign digital companies at a wider scale. The preference for using a minimum tax is that it would serve the function of a license to operate in the market territory, while still being an income tax, unlike exclusive taxes, which are not income taxes, but taxes levied on whatever is used to determine the tax presumption.

On a different note, rebuttable presumptions are closely related to alternative taxes, which can be defined as taxes that allow for multiple ways of calculating the tax base, as opposed to nonalternative taxes, which do not contemplate optional methods of tax assessment. Given the complexity of digital business models and their disparity with both legal and economic structures, it would be preferable to design a tax that comprises alternative methods of tax assessment, which may be useful for tailoring the tax liability to the circumstances of the digital business model and to the specific industry.

Similarly, presumptive digital taxes should be determined individually because tax liabilities are significantly high—especially if the current thresholds are kept, which greatly reduces the number of taxpayers—as are the associated costs of tax administration. Under collective assessment, the tax administration establishes presumptive income for groups of taxpayers, corresponding to different activities, and assigns each taxpayer to a group, which determines the taxpayer's tax liability. Although collective assessment has the advantage of administrative simplicity, the individual assessment method has the advantage of greater accuracy, which should prevail when creating new taxing rights. Indeed, DSTs are not applied by groups, which is even less accurate than collective assessment. Amount A would apply collective assessment to define different thresholds and fixed percentages by groups, but it is not clear whether taxpayers would be given the opportunity to contest the classification of their business activity, which in some countries can be done in court. In sum, individual assessment should replace collective assessment when establishing presumptive income from digital business models, particularly since, under individual assessment, taxpayers can negotiate with tax administrations or appeal through the judicial system, which could lead to income taxation and increased tax compliance.

Another aspect that needs to be analyzed is the degree of discretion that presumptive methods allow tax officials. Some methods are quite mechanical, allowing no discretion, while others involve a high degree of discretion for the agent applying them. Turnover taxes, like digital services taxes and the Unified Approach, are applied mechanically and do not allow for any discretion, which is aligned with collective assessment and the use of irrebuttable presumptions. As explained, these traits are not the most appropriate ones for newly created taxing rights on digital activities. They should be replaced by rebuttable presumptions, individual assessments, and discretionary application to limit the risk of arbitrary action on the part of tax administrations, while introducing some flexibility for negotiation between foreign digital companies and market jurisdictions. Unless tax measures and initiatives are revised in this direction and some compromise is reached, the application of presumptive digital taxes will depend entirely on effective tax collection and tax enforcement mechanisms, without any involvement of taxpayers' voluntary compliance. This approach may ultimately result in digital multinationals discontinuing their business operations in certain countries solely for economic reasons.

Recently, the United States has suggested that the Unified Approach may be used as a safe harbor, leaving to digital multinationals the decision on whether or not to adhere to it. This approach is different from optional taxation. Traditionally, optional taxes have allowed taxpayers to choose between tax assessment methods, including presumptive ones. For example, the taxpayer may only be allowed to choose if certain requirements (recordkeeping) are met and the tax administration authorizes the taxpayer's option; alternatively, the tax administration may be given the power to choose the applicable method. These alternatives are usually considered appropriate for a context where tax administrations apply residence taxation and the option affects the choice of tax assessment method, but the tax is levied either way, irrespective of the method chosen. In contrast, the safe harbor approach has a radically different meaning and tax implications. Basically, it would affect the exercise of the market jurisdiction's taxing right itself and would give taxpayers the power to opt out of application of the taxing right, turning the Unified Approach into a voluntary tax, only applicable if companies want to benefit from both mandatory, time-limited, and binding dispute resolution mechanisms and a more formulaic approach to transfer pricing. This voluntary safe harbor approach would be aligned with traditional tax theory principles.

Effective Tax Collection of Digital Taxes

Tax collection is, by far, the most challenging phase of tax administration, especially for digital transactions involving nonresidents, which bear a higher tax evasion risk as a result of the greater difficulty of using traditional local tax enforcement mechanisms to reach residents in other countries. For the purpose of this section, tax collection refers to any mechanism that secures payment of the tax liability during the voluntary period of compliance. Afterward, once the voluntary period has expired, any further action aimed at securing payment of the pending tax liability is considered tax enforcement. Accordingly, tax collection may comprise direct tax payment by the taxpayer or tax withholding and subsequent payment by a tax agent, usually the payor (customer, buyer, employer, financial institution, intermediary), independent of the timing, periodicity, and installment schedules of such tax payments, which are conditioned by the government's need for liquidity to meet its financial obligations.

Given the lack of a physical presence of foreign digital companies in market jurisdictions, the option of direct tax payment may not be the most appropriate. Absent voluntary tax compliance, the options for tax recovery once the income has been paid out abroad are minimal, and effectiveness of tax enforcement mechanisms is limited. Therefore, applying tax withholding seems to be the most promising mechanism for collecting taxes from foreign digital companies, but it is necessary to establish the scope of digital transactions subject to withholding and the identity of the tax agents. In this regard, some lessons may be drawn from the experience of applying withholding to indirect taxation of digital services. For instance, in B2C transactions, nonresident digital suppliers act as withholding agents of the indirect tax that needs to be paid to the tax administration of the market jurisdiction. This situation creates a greater incentive for tax evasion, since withheld indirect taxes derive from transactions with consumers, who are much harder to trace and to monitor. In contrast, in B2B transactions, the reverse charge mechanism applies, and resident customers must withhold the output indirect tax (VAT) and declare in their VAT returns both their purchases (input VAT) and their suppliers' sales (withheld output VAT), which offset each other from a cash payment viewpoint, minimizing the risk of tax evasion.

The situation is the opposite for direct taxation at source of digital businesses, since foreign digital companies are not withholding agents, but, instead, are taxpayers. In B2B transactions, corporate customers resident in the market jurisdiction would act as withholding agents and would apply tax withholdings on digital transactions. Similarly, local digital platforms, acting as distributors or intermediaries in the territory, would act as withholding agents on behalf of the nonresident digital suppliers. Contrary to the comprehensive B2B withholding mechanism, B2C digital transactions raise some issues. For example, engaging consumers to act as withholding agents is not a practicable option, since it would impose a disproportionate burden on them, and tax compliance would be extremely hard to monitor, at least using conventional tax tools. These limitations create an opportunity for foreign digital companies conducting B2C transactions not only to evade direct taxes at source but also to misappropriate input indirect taxes collected from consumers. The rampant use of technology and the digital nature of transactions may help to solve this situation in the near future. For example, technology-enabled automated withholding software does not require consumer intervention to apply and process tax withholdings on merchants.

Meanwhile, until technology enables the application of the B2B withholding mechanism to B2C digital transactions, alternative tax-withholding agents may be needed to collect taxes from nonresident digital suppliers. To this end, tax policy legislators should focus their attention on the internet (digital communication, distribution channel) and on the financial sector (digital payment). Although some digital payments do not require the intervention of traditional financial institutions (cryptocurrencies, virtual currencies, stored-value cards), the majority of digital payments are channeled through banks and credit card companies, since most users still earn their income outside the internet and receive their salary through banks. Only those users whose economy relies exclusively on digital payment methods that are outside the traditional financial sector may escape such financial sector control. Having said this, engaging the financial sector as withholding agent, at least for B2C digital transactions, would help to overcome the constraints described, since financial institutions have full control over outbound payments and may easily apply withholding on qualifying outbound transfers of funds. Indeed, this alternative could potentially be applicable to all types of digital transactions (B2C, B2B, P2P, business-to-government [B2G]), which would facilitate taxing other streams of digital income (P2P lending). Unfortunately, the financial sector is not always willing or eager to collaborate on tax enforcement tasks (applying tax withholdings), because they fear losing clients to financial institutions located abroad that may not abide by the same national legal duties or simply not be within their scope. Therefore, any effort in this direction should be at the global level and within the scope of the G-20 mandate to align the national interests of worldwide governments under a common tax framework.

Tax Enforcement of Digital Tax Claims

Taxpayers do not fear tax audit; taxpayers fear effective tax enforcement, which may ultimately result in loss of assets (property seizure, funds freeze, judicial foreclosure) and loss of freedom (imprisonment). Such penalties are effectively implemented in the country where assets are located and where taxpayers have their tax residence and are physically present. Furthermore, tax enforcement has much higher success rates for resident taxpayers, since they can be identified and located more easily, and information on their assets and execution procedures is readily available (bank account freeze, tax litigation, property seizure, lien on assets, judicial foreclosure), which contrasts with the bureaucratic procedures for exchange of information and with the burdensome processes for cross-border execution. Hence, we should not be surprised that tax evasion is not exclusively a domestic issue; indeed, it is quite the opposite.

Accordingly, most digital economy–related tax evasion schemes involve nonresident suppliers, which means that any enforcement action requires assistance from the other countries where the noncompliant taxpayer is a tax resident or its assets are located. Usually, most jurisdictions tend to provide administrative and judicial cooperation to other countries in the assessment and collection of taxes, ranging from the exchange of information, including even automatic exchanges, to the recovery of foreign tax claims. However, enforcement of the tax claims of market jurisdictions based on new nexus and profit attribution rules may not be so well received, especially by residence countries where digital multinationals are domiciled. The explanation is that traditional cross-border tax cooperation does not normally pose any conflicting tax claims between the two jurisdictions (the one requesting assistance and the one providing assistance), since taxing rights are founded on internationally accepted tax theory principles, and requests for cooperation are supported by legal instruments (Convention on Mutual Administrative Assistance in Tax Matters, tax treaties, exchange of information agreements, multilateral conventions for the recognition and enforcement of foreign judgments). Therefore, providing tax assistance to a foreign country does not undermine residence-based taxing rights, and, most of the time, such cooperation is not left to the discretion of tax authorities but, instead, is mandated by agreed legal instruments.

Under the new digital scenario and assuming no amendments are made to the existing legal instruments, which would require approval by participating jurisdictions, any request for international tax cooperation to enforce abroad tax claims arising from newly created taxing rights based on new and revised nexus and profit attribution rules (DSTs, significant economic presence, Amount A of the Unified Approach, virtual service permanent establishment, equalization levies) would most probably result in a denial of assistance if the country receiving the request is the country of tax residence of the digital company, as a consequence of the conflicting tax claims of both jurisdictions. Such a negative response would be logical given that assisting the market jurisdiction would go against the country's residence-based taxing rights, either because the residence country would be forced to grant unilateral tax relief to the taxpayer affected by the enforced compliance, which would reduce its national tax revenue base, or because it would facilitate and enable double taxation of its resident taxpayer, indirectly harming its national economy. Moreover, no obligation to provide the assistance would exist, since the scope of application of existing legal instruments would not cover such new tax claims (tax treaties cover income-based taxes, not revenue-based taxes). The only scenario where such tax assistance might be provided would be if the jurisdiction receiving the request is not the residence country of the digital company, but assets (including bank accounts) are still located therein and the market country's tax authorities are aiming to recover their tax claims by realizing such assets. Without an exchange of information from residence countries, it would be very difficult to identify the assets and their foreign location. Even so, in the absence of any legal obligation, most countries would be reluctant to intervene, since they would be indirectly harming their foreign investors and, consequently, their reputation and ability to attract foreign direct investment, without any legal basis for it or benefit in return.

Therefore, market jurisdictions' tax claims arising from newly created taxing rights based on new and revised nexus and profit allocation rules would hardly benefit from cross-border tax assistance from foreign countries, especially from those where the digital companies affected by the request are tax residents. As a consequence, if digital taxes are finally implemented, enforcement will depend on market jurisdictions' capabilities to monitor and control the digital activity happening within their borders. Once tax collection mechanisms fail, the only enforcement alternative left will be to ban any future digital activity of the noncompliant foreign digital supplier in the territory; such a ban would require cooperation between tax administrations and ISPs that control access and digital activity in the country. Internet access would be suspended until pending tax claims are satisfied. From a technical perspective, such an enforcement measure is fully practicable, and nowadays it is used to prevent criminal activities as well as to screen certain digital content (block sites).

Bibliography

Ainsworth, Richard, Musaad Alwohaibi, Andrew Leahey, Yijin Li, and Haseena Rahman. 2020a. "Afghanistan's New VAT, Part 1: Invoice Matching or a Unitary Digital Invoice." *Tax Notes International* 100 (November 30, 2020).

Ainsworth, Richard, Musaad Alwohaibi, Andrew Leahey, Yijin Li, and Haseena Rahman. 2020b. "Afghanistan's New VAT, Part 2: Lessons from South Korea, China, and India's Automation Efforts." *Tax Notes International* 100 (December 7, 2020).

Ainsworth, Richard, and Chang Che. 2019. "Data First—Tax Next: How Fiji's Technology Can Improve New Zealand's 'Netflix Tax' (Electronic Marketplaces) Part 3." *Tax Notes International* 95 (1249): 1249–83.

Ainsworth, Richard, and Xiuyuan (Tony) Hu. 2020. "A Proposal for Taxing Cryptocurrency in the Midst of the COVID-19 Pandemic." *Tax Notes International* 98 (8): 921–29.

Ba, El Hadji Dialigue. 2019. *Le droit fiscal à l´épreuve de la mondialisation: La réglementation des prix de transfert au Sénégal*. Riga: Éditions Universitaires Européennes.

Bird, Richard, and Milka Casanegra de Jantscher. 1992. *Improving Tax Administration in Developing Countries*. Washington, DC: International Monetary Fund.

Bird, Richard, and Sally Wallace. 2003. "Is It Really So Hard to Tax the Hard-to-Tax? The Context and Role of Presumptive Taxes." In *Taxing the Hard-to-Tax: Lessons from Theory and Practice*, Contributions to Economic Analysis vol. 268, edited by James Alm, Jorge Martinez-Vazquez, and Sally Wallace. Somerville, MA: Emerald Publishing Limited.

Bulutoglu, Kenan. 1995. "Presumptive Taxation." In *Tax Policy Handbook*, edited by Parthasarathi Shome. Washington, DC: International Monetary Fund.

Clavey, Colin, Jonathan Leigh Pemberton, Jan Loeprick, and Marinus Verhoeven. 2019. "International Tax Reform, Digitalization, and Developing Economies." MTI Discussion Paper 16, Macroeconomics, Trade, and Investment Global Practice, World Bank Group, Washington, DC.

Junquera-Varela, Raúl Félix, Rajul Awasthi, Oleksii Balabushko, and Alma Nurshaikhova. 2019. "Thinking Strategically about Revenue Administration Reform: The Creation of Integrated, Autonomous Revenue Bodies—Policy Note." Governance Discussion Paper 4, World Bank Group, Washington, DC.

Junquera-Varela, Raúl Félix, Marijn Verhoeven, Gangadhar P. Shukla, Bernard Haven, Rajul Awasthi, and Blanca Moreno-Dodson. 2017. *Strengthening Domestic Resource Mobilization: Moving from Theory to Practice in Low- and Middle-Income Countries*. Directions in Development—Public Sector Governance. Washington, DC: World Bank.

Kaeser, Christian, Jeffrey Owens, and Sam Sim. 2019. "Going the Way of the Polaroid: Digital Taxation and the End of the Arm's Length Principle?" *Tax Notes International* 95 (3): 211–19.

Lapidoth, Arye. 1977. *The Use of Estimation for the Assessment of Taxable Business Income (with Special Emphasis on the Problems of Taxing Small Business)*. Selected Monographs on Taxation, Harvard Law School International Tax Program. Cambridge, MA: Harvard Law School; Amsterdam: International Bureau of Fiscal Documentation.

Le, Tuan Minh, Blanca Moreno-Dodson, and Nihal Bayraktar. 2012. "Tax Capacity and Tax Effort: Extended Cross-Country Analysis from 1994 to 2009." Policy Research Working Paper WPS6252, World Bank Group, Washington, DC.

Lucas-Mas, Mayra Olivia. 2008. *Los sistemas de precios de transferencia en perspectiva impositiva y aduanera: Análisis y posibles vías de conciliación*. Madrid: Instituto de Estudios Fiscales, Ministerio de Economía y Hacienda.

Rajaraman, Indira. 1995. "Presumptive Direct Taxation: Lessons from Experience in Developing Countries." *Economic and Political Weekly* 30 (18-19): 1103–24.

Schenk, Alan, and Oliver Oldman. 2007. *Value Added Tax: A Comparative Approach*. New York: Cambridge University Press.

Surrey, Stanley. 1958. "Tax Administration in Underdeveloped Countries." *University of Miami Law Review* 12 (2): 158–88.

Tanzi, Vito, and Milka Casanegra de Jantscher. 1987. "Presumptive Income Taxation: Administrative, Efficiency, and Equity Aspects." IMF Working Paper, International Monetary Fund, Washington, DC.

Thuronyi, Victor. 1996. "Presumptive Taxation." In *Tax Law Design and Drafting*, vol. 1, ch. 12. Washington, DC: International Monetary Fund.

Zolt, Eric. 2017. "Tax Incentives in Developing Countries: Maximizing the Benefits and Minimizing the Costs." In *United Nations Handbook on Selected Issues in Protecting the Tax Base of Developing Countries*, edited by Alexander Trepelkov, Harry Tonino, and Dominika Halka, ch. 9. New York: United Nations.

CHAPTER 7

Tax Proposal for Taxing the Digital Economy

So far, we have analyzed the tax-disruptive aspects of digital business models, the application of tax principles to taxing the digital economy, and the implications of economic, legal, tax policy, and tax administration perspectives. This chapter presents a proposal for taxing the digital economy, based on the creation of a specialized global internet tax agency (GITA), which would be entrusted with supporting countries in administering a new digital data tax (DDT). It explains and analyzes the defining elements of this original tax proposal, which would overcome the challenges posed by current tax measures and initiatives, while abiding by traditional tax theory.

Creation of a New Global Internet Tax Agency

In the absence of an international tax legal system and a global tax authority, the digital debate comes down to a clash of national economic interests, where market countries claim new taxing rights at the expense of eroding the tax bases of residence countries. In this context, we propose the creation of a specialized global internet tax agency, which would be responsible for providing tax administration technical support to all jurisdictions that may choose to enact and implement a digital data tax in their territories (box 7.1). Given that the digital economy is a global phenomenon and internet users operate worldwide, national tax authorities would need to gain access to information on digital transactions and internet activity to administer the new DDT. The GITA would provide such support, along with assistance in tax administration matters. Furthermore, the GITA's information resources would prove useful for administering indirect taxes on digital transactions (value added tax [VAT]/goods and services tax [GST] on digital services, tariffs on the trade of digital goods in case the World Trade Organization ban is eventually lifted), especially in low-tax-capacity countries, where access to information and technical expertise are limited.

The decision to introduce a new DDT would be made at the national level, so each country would choose whether or not to apply it. The GITA would provide technical

---

Box 7.1 Comparison between the Digital Data Tax Proposal and Federal Schemes

The proposed digital data tax (DDT) bears a resemblance to "equalization" schemes in federal countries. Such schemes must, in effect, always be run by the federal government, but they usually require the agreement of subnational governments on how the size of the pool is determined and especially on how it is allocated. Such agreement is difficult to obtain, even within a country, which is why some scholars are skeptical about the viability of achieving the required degree of consensus among nations. In fact, if the functioning of such a structure is challenging within a federal context, it is even more challenging within the global context, where incentives are diffused, not just between resident countries and market participation economies but also within each group of countries. Once broad agreement on creating such an institution is reached, other even more thorny questions regarding financing, governance structure, or creation of a work plan risk a clash of opposing ideas that will threaten its ability to function.

The proposed global internet tax agency (GITA) also has a lot in common with the United States Multistate Tax Commission (MTC). Both are intergovernmental tax agencies whose mission is to promote uniform and consistent tax policy and administration among their members, to assist taxpayers in achieving compliance, and to advocate for tax sovereignty in the development of tax policy. However, some scholars do not think that the MTC's structure is appropriate for the GITA. They note that the existence of the MTC does not preclude the freedom of choice or design of state tax policy. In particular, the design of a range of issues—specifically the type of taxes, tax rates, and tax incentives—is not aligned with the proposed functions and responsibilities of a GITA, which will make it difficult for the GITA to handle DDT.

---

support and information to countries; in some cases, upon request and tax delegation, it also could assist in some tax administrative matters. Yet the DDT would be levied on all internet users with a significant digital presence (SDP) in the country, which would capture both the domestic and the international digital economy. It would be assessed on the basis of contracted internet bandwidth and be allocated to market jurisdictions according to their volume of internet data inflows.

The responsibilities of the GITA would be determined by each country's delegation, including, but not limited to, the following:

- Monitoring worldwide internet activity
- Compiling in a single database all tax-relevant data on digital transactions
- Centralizing all tax registration procedures from internet businesses and customers in a unique official online portal

- Characterizing income from digital business models
- Assessing digital taxing rights by jurisdiction
- Coordinating with national tax authorities and internet service providers (ISPs) on collection and enforcement of the DDT
- Allocating to market jurisdictions the assigned share of tax revenues from the DDT
- Assisting national tax authorities in resolving any DDT-related tax disputes
- Providing technical assistance to low-tax-capacity countries in tax policy and tax administration of digital taxes other than the DDT
- Acting as a clearinghouse between countries on the basis of the previous allocation of DDT revenues worldwide
- Supervising the compliance of transfers of DDT revenues between countries
- Auditing the tax practices of countries administering the DDT.

National tax authorities would perform tax administration functions in application of the new DDT within their respective jurisdictions and in connection with their resident taxpayers on the basis of all tax-relevant information provided by the GITA. In this sense, national tax authorities would retain and manage tax responsibilities related to the following:

- Collecting DDT voluntary payments and withholdings
- Processing DDT refund claims
- Auditing DDT taxpayers and tax agents
- Enforcing all other DDT tax obligations.

This technically specialized agency would have a mandate from all member countries to provide tax support and to coordinate the exchange of information with financial institutions and internet service providers (tier-1 through tier-3 ISPs). It would be equipped with all of the necessary means, resources, and powers to fulfill this mission. Moreover, similar to the Internet Corporation for Assigned Names and Numbers (ICANN) and the Internet Engineering Task Force (IETF), the GITA would be fully independent and free from any kind of national, regional, and political interference. At the same time, it would need to have the full support of the global community and should be created under the auspices of the United Nations (UN) as a new specialized agency in charge of addressing the tax challenges posed by digitalization of the economy.

As part of the United Nations, the GITA would benefit from the UN institutional network, technical expertise, and resources. Even more important, the United Nations would ensure that all countries join as members and participate on a truly equal footing, which would guarantee the agency's political neutrality and the global community's support. Indeed, no other international organization is better positioned than the United Nations to lead this global initiative: the United Nations brings together the entire international community and contributes the experience and infrastructure of its specialized agencies (International Monetary Fund, International

Telecommunication Union, World Bank Group), which will prove decisive in fulfilling the missions of this new agency.

The GITA would have three main missions:

- To provide technical support and coordination in the tax administration of the new digital data tax
- To provide technical assistance to low-tax-capacity countries in the administration of indirect taxes on the digital economy (VAT/ GST on digital services)
- To serve as a global registry of all digital economy–related information that facilitates cross-border administration and monitoring of taxable internet activity.

To fulfill these missions, financial sector institutions (banks, credit card companies, insurance companies) would have to cooperate fully with national tax authorities and with the GITA to ensure that all financial transactions connected to digital activities are characterized properly and subject to tax withholding, if needed. These institutions would also need to support countries in the collection of digital taxes from business-to-consumer (B2C) transactions and assist the GITA and ISPs in the enforcement of pending tax claims from the DDT.

In order to process online payments directly or through payment platforms, financial institutions would require internet users conducting online business operations

---

Box 7.2 Previous Proposals for Creating a Global Tax Authority

Article 82 of the United Nations Convention on the Law of the Sea obligates coastal states to make payments to a United Nations body called the International Seabed Authority for the exploitation of nonliving resources of the extended continental shelf beyond 200 nautical miles. To date, Article 82 has not been triggered, although it may be soon.

Vito Tanzi proposed creating a world tax authority (WTA), a concept that evolved over time. Initially, in 1988, Tanzi proposed that the WTA would have the power to levy taxes on the citizens of sovereign countries (Tanzi 1988). Later, in 1999, domestic tax problems were excluded from the list of WTA responsibilities, which were conceived as providing technical assistance, especially to poorer countries when they require it, as, for example, in their dealings with multinational corporations (Tanzi 1999). The GITA resembles the latter version of WTA more than the former.

Richard Ainsworth and Xiuyuan (Tony) Hu proposed creating a supranational tax authority in charge of taxing cryptocurrencies. El Hadji Dialigue Ba (Ba 2019) proposed creating a global transfer pricing observatory. French president Jacques Chirac proposed creating a global tax system to fund development projects that might include a tax on aviation and maritime shipping fuel or a tax on the worldwide sale of airplane tickets. Finally, the European Union proposed imposing a "Tobin tax" on international currency exchanges, an idea that has recently reemerged from the past and been adopted by some countries (Spain).

(digital supplies and services) and economic activities over the internet (virtual financial services, online gambling, software licensing, crowdfunding) to provide both their internet protocol (IP) address and their new internet tax identification number (ITIN), which the GITA would assign to them at the time of registration. Financial institutions would then share this additional set of banking data with national tax authorities and with the GITA, via the new automatic exchange of information (AEOI) global standard currently in place or through any other legal mechanism (such as the Foreign Account Tax Compliance Act). This information would be cross-checked and matched with information that ISPs provide on the use of internet bandwidth of registered internet users, for DDT assessment purposes.

This new proposal for creating a GITA is radically different from previous proposals that advocated creating a global tax authority in charge of administering its own taxing rights with autonomous powers (box 7.2). Unlike those proposals, the GITA would only provide specialized technical support upon request to assist countries in administering a new DDT and any other digital taxes they have introduced.

Introduction of a New Digital Data Tax

Internet businesses with significant digital activity require sufficient server bandwidth to ensure that their websites do not crash or slow down and can absorb internet traffic flow. Therefore, while internet data have a value, transferring or receiving data has a cost, derived from paying servers for internet bandwidth (box 7.3). This cost increases

---

Box 7.3 Bandwidth Explained

Bandwidth describes the maximum data transfer rate of a network or internet connection. It measures how much data can be sent over a specific connection in a given amount of time. While bandwidth is used to describe network speeds, it does not measure how fast bits of data move from one location to another. Since data packets travel over electronic or fiber optic cables, the speed of each bit transferred is negligible. Instead, bandwidth measures how much data can flow through a specific connection at one time.

When visualizing bandwidth, it may help to think of a network connection as a tube and each bit of data as a grain of sand. If you pour a large amount of sand into a skinny tube, it will take a long time for the sand to flow through it. If you pour the same amount of sand through a wide tube, the sand will flow through the tube much faster. Similarly, a download will finish much faster when you have a high-bandwidth connection rather than a low-bandwidth connection.

Data often flow over multiple network connections, which means that the connection with the smallest bandwidth acts as a bottleneck. Generally, the internet backbone and connections between servers have the most bandwidth, so they rarely become bottlenecks. The most common internet bottleneck is the connection to an internet service provider.

---

proportionally to bandwidth capacity, which is only justified if the increase in internet traffic creates more value for the internet business. Why would internet businesses incur server bandwidth costs if they were not making money from internet traffic?

Based on this assumption, market jurisdictions are encouraged to explore introducing a digital license-type tax on foreign digital suppliers that wish to access and operate remotely in their digital markets, which is the backbone of our DDT proposal (box 7.4). The DDT would consist of two components, one acting as a toll tax and one acting as a service charge for contracted internet bandwidth (in the global DDT) or for significant digital presence (in national DDTs). Such a DDT would not be a presumptive income tax[1] in any manner: source income taxation of nonresident companies without a physical presence is not compatible with traditional tax theory principles. The DDT would overcome this obstacle by operating as a digital license-type tax that would be deductible as a business operating cost in the residence jurisdiction of the digital supplier. It would not be creditable, as income taxes usually are. The DDT also would be modulated depending on the degree of significant digital presence.

The global DDT would be introduced at a national level[2] as a newly created stand-alone[3] tax that would be levied on all internet users with a significant digital presence in the jurisdiction. SDP would be based on the volume of internet data flow with the territory, measured by two indicators, which would also serve as allocation keys for distributing global DDT revenues among market jurisdictions: (a) the number of digital transactions conducted with users physically located in the territory and (b) the number of visits to the online websites from users physically located in the country. The first indicator aims to measure the economic activity arising from the paid supply of digital content and digital services (digital business models as well as the following tax-disruptive digital business models, detailed in table 2.3 in chapter 2: sale of nonuser digital content, licensing of digital content, subscription to digital content, virtual banking, virtual insurance, online gambling, online e-commerce marketplace). The second indicator targets the economic activity arising from the monetization of user-related data and content contributed in exchange for free access to digital content and digital platforms (the remaining tax-disruptive digital business models: sale of user-related data and user-contributed digital content, online user-targeted advertising, sale of user-related goodwill as part of the sale of a digital business). Therefore, the new DDT would capture the digital presence of domestic and foreign internet users operating in market jurisdictions without a physical presence. The defining trait of such targeted users is their monetization-oriented economic activity in the form of a digital business model, regardless of whether they end up generating income or not and irrespective of whether they operate the business model as legal entities or as individuals.

The DDT would not be a presumptive income tax. It would be a digital license-type tax, which is totally different. The former assumes the existence of some sort of income, while the latter does not necessarily require any income (the DDT would tax contracted internet data bandwidth, irrespective of whether it is effectively used or not or whether any income is generated or not from such use), as happens with business licenses and

Box 7.4 Comparison of the Proposed Digital Data Tax to a Bit Tax

The digital data tax (DDT) bears some resemblance to the groundbreaking bit tax, which was proposed by visionary tax expert Arthur Cordell and originally presented in 1995 as a form of consumption tax that would tax the flows of digital information between global networks (Cordell 1996, 1997). It would apply to the number of computer bits of information received by the user through the intermediary of the internet service provider (ISP). Later in 1999, the United Nations Development Programme included in the *Human Development Report* a simplified version of the bit tax that was limited to taxing internet e-mail (UNDP 1999).

In 2000, several countries, including Australia and Canada, as well as the European Union rejected the bit tax. The European Union argued that a bit tax would not be in accordance with basic principles of international taxation. Canada stated that the concept of a transaction tax on the flow of electronic information, without regard to the value of that information, could create economic anomalies and impede the growth of electronic commerce. For example, valuable data contained in a relatively small volume of digital information would, under a bit tax, be subject to a correspondingly small tax, while the transfer of a movie, involving large amounts of digital information, would be subject to a large bit tax. Even the Organisation for Economic Co-operation and Development (OECD), in 2014, considered a bit tax based on the volume of bandwidth used by multinationals' websites, but later abandoned it. Similarly, Hungary's bit tax of Ft 150 (US$0.60) per gigabyte of data traffic, introduced in 2014, attracted massive protests and was ultimately repealed. For all of these reasons, the bit tax proposal was abandoned.

The DDT proposal aims to overcome the deficiencies and weaknesses of the bit tax and significantly differs from it in various aspects:

- The DDT would not depend on the amount of digital data (bits) sent via the internet, but instead on the contracted internet bandwidth, irrespective of whether such capacity is used or not, which is much easier to assess and to implement (the DDT would be levied by ISPs at the time of contracting the internet bandwidth, even if not one single bit is later sent via the internet).
- The DDT would only apply to internet users conducting business online, not to private users, as the bit tax would have done.
- The DDT would be in accordance with the basic principles of international taxation since taxpayers would receive a benefit in return—they would gain access to the digital market of a given jurisdiction to conduct business remotely—in contrast to the bit tax, which would apply without any benefit in return.

other operating business costs and investments. The key would be the intention to conduct business, similar to a lease or rental of office space, which is a cost for any company that intends to conduct business, even if, at the end, no profits are generated or the physical facilities are not used. In this sense, the DDT would be a fixed cost for any internet user who intends to operate a digital business model in a given country. It would operate as a mandatory toll tax to use the internet "highways" to access the "digital market" of a market jurisdiction and be levied according to the degree of significant digital presence. Since it would not be an income tax, it would not be creditable, but it might be deductible as a business operating expense if residence countries allow it.

Thus the DDT would be characterized as a digital license-type tax (not presumptive, since presumptive taxation only applies to income taxes), which would be assessed on the basis of the global volume of contracted internet bandwidth and on having internet access to a certain number of market jurisdictions and, therefore, having a significant digital presence therein. This approach would incorporate a new notion of digital protection, arising from the mandatory authorization required from national telecommunication authorities to operate in their territories in exchange for a license-type tax, which would include a toll tax as the national component of it. Each country would be able to establish the amount of toll tax, and the tax revenues from it would belong to each jurisdiction granting internet access. This would be one of the two components of the tax base used to calculate DDT liability. The other component would be the amount of internet bandwidth contracted with ISPs, which would follow a proportional tax rate structure; internet users would be taxed according to their need for internet capacity. Such a tax rate schedule would be agreed upon yearly by all GITA member countries, subject to previous consultation with other relevant internet actors (ISPs, financial sector entities). Different internet bandwidth thresholds could be set to distinguish between small and medium internet businesses and large internet multinationals, the latter being subject to a progressive tax rate schedule, more exhaustive monitoring based on enhanced risk assessment, and reinforced tax enforcement mechanisms by tax authorities in connection with other tax obligations (tax withholding agents for VAT on business-to-business [B2B] transactions, foreign suppliers for VAT on B2C transactions).

Alternatively, if the GITA is not created immediately, the digital data tax could also be introduced unilaterally and implemented by national tax authorities, which could be done as either an interim or a permanent measure. Obviously, this option would involve changing the design of the DDT somewhat to overcome the lack of information on the global amount of internet bandwidth contracted, which is usually only known by the local or regional ISP of the internet user, which in most cases is located outside the market jurisdiction. At the same time, this option would allow countries to have exclusive control over the entire tax administration of the DDT. They would not need to wait for the GITA to calculate and allocate each country's share of the global amount of contracted internet bandwidth, and they would not need to operate as a clearinghouse.

Therefore, the national version of the DDT, without intervention of the GITA, would have two components. The first one would be a toll tax for gaining internet access to the country, which has already been discussed. The second one would be a measure of the size of the digital presence. It would be assessed on the basis of the two indicators previously used as allocation keys and now serving as tax bases: (a) the number of digital transactions conducted with users physically located in the territory and (b) the number of visits to online websites from users physically located in the country. This second component would be calculated differently from country to country, depending on the weight assigned to each indicator. Certain tax thresholds could be introduced to exempt internet users without a significant digital presence in the taxing jurisdiction (low volume of digital transactions, small number of visits). Certain types of users also could be exempted from the entire DDT or any of its two components, like those acting as mere contributors of digital content without deriving any economic gain from digital activities (bloggers, nonprofit organization sites, charities, crowdsourcing sites) or public entities (government sites, public universities, public service initiatives), unless they use the internet to collect revenue or for any other monetization strategy that may generate value for them.

Given that the DDT aims to capture a significant digital presence, which requires some kind of website or web page through which internet users interact, the DDT would initially be assessed for those internet users that contract not only internet bandwidth and servers but also web-hosting services associated with a domain name. This assessment would require any of the two DDT modalities (global or national) to establish cooperation mechanisms between the tax authorities or the GITA and web-hosting providers and ICANN. This multiparty system would allow greater control of internet presence, especially for tax monitoring within a jurisdiction and for tax enforcement in case of noncompliant taxpayers, which would facilitate banning their online websites. As a disadvantage, focusing on internet businesses operating through websites may make it more difficult to detect other internet users whose businesses do not rely on online websites, such as digital entrepreneurs concluding contracts over the internet or digital nomads providing high-value services over e-mail (information technology consultancy services, legal services, financial advisory services, accounting services), without any need for having special servers or transferring high volumes of digital data. In these cases, their digital presence would be registered, but not taxed, by the mandatory registration procedure under the global version of the DDT.

Another important difference between the global DDT version (which involves the GITA) and the national DDT version is that only the global version applies the fractional apportionment method for allocating and distributing to member jurisdictions the tax revenues from the contracted internet bandwidth component of the global DDT; these tasks can only be coordinated by the GITA, given its global reach. This same constraint prevents national tax authorities from using contracted internet bandwidth as the tax base of national DDTs, since such information is not readily available to national tax authorities from international ISPs. If the DDT is implemented unilaterally without global coordination, residence countries would not grant tax relief to their tax-resident taxpayers subject to one or more foreign DDTs as a result of their online business operations abroad. However, if a global DDT is applied by national tax authorities and supported by the GITA, then member countries could be required to provide tax relief in the form of a tax credit or a tax deduction. Deduction would probably be the preferred choice, allowing internet business users to deduct as a business operating expense the global DDT paid (box 7.5).

Any of the two DDT modalities shown in figure 7.1 would replace turnover-based taxes (digital services taxes, equalization levies) and tax initiatives aimed at creating direct taxing rights in favor of market jurisdictions for digital activity conducted within their borders (Amount A of the OECD's Unified Approach). The DDT also would take into account all types of digital transactions (B2B, B2C, business-to-government [B2G], peer-to-peer [P2P]), either for global allocation of DDT by the GITA or as a tax base for national DDT assessment. Indeed, most B2B and B2C transactions are conducted via websites or web pages, even when digital content may also be delivered digitally via other channels (e-mail).

Box 7.5 Would the Digital Data Tax Be Creditable?

Some scholars have stressed the importance of the digital data tax (DDT) being creditable. However, given that the DDT is not an income tax, not even a presumptive one, the option for tax credit is very limited. This trade-off requires a three-way compromise. For example, the fact that the DDT would not be creditable against residence taxation may prompt multinational enterprises to oppose it, as happens with current digital taxes (digital services taxes, equalization levies). In contrast, if the DDT were fully creditable, then residence jurisdictions would be the ones to fight it, since they would have to absorb the entire DDT, which would erode their tax base, as suggested by current proposals (Unified Approach). Therefore, the half-way compromise would be to stress that the DDT is not an income tax (because traditional tax theory principles do not support income taxation by source countries without a brick-and-mortar permanent establishment), so residence jurisdictions would not have to give away part of their tax base (via income tax credits). At the same time, a new taxing right would be recognized for market jurisdictions in the form of a digital license-type tax, which would be tax deductible as an operating expense by multinational enterprises against their income taxes back in their residence countries.

Consequently, nobody would win, which is the best possible compromise:

- Multinational enterprises would not be subject to a full income tax (or, even worse, to a presumptive turnover-based version of it), which most probably would not be creditable. Instead, they would be subject to the DDT, which would be tax deductible.
- Market jurisdictions would get substantial revenues from the DDT, as shown in the case study presented later in this chapter.
- Residence countries would not surrender taxing rights, but would grant a tax deduction for DDT as an operating cost.

To sum up, the DDT proposal offers the best compromise out of all current digital taxes and tax initiatives, since it takes into account not only the interests of both source and residence countries, but also the interests of digital multinationals.

Figure 7.1 Tax Design of Global and National Modalities of Digital Data Tax

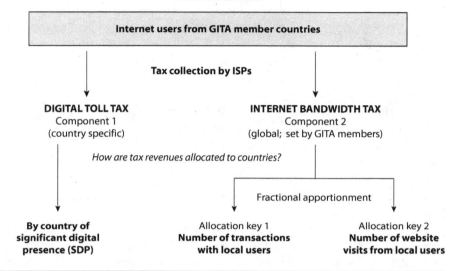

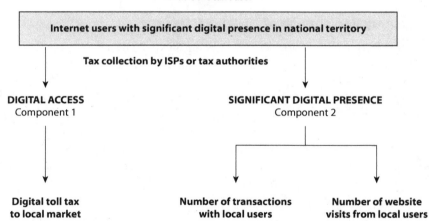

Source: Original figure for this publication.
Note: GITA = global internet tax agency; ISP = internet service provider.

This proposal would assign value to binary-code (digital) data transferred over the internet. In some way, internet bandwidth is the new soil. Historically, presumptive taxation was first used in ancient Egypt, where farmers were taxed based on the surface area they cultivated, not on their actual harvested crops, plus a variable element like the annually changing water level of the Nile River. Similarly, even if the DDT is not a presumptive tax, it operates in the same way in some aspects: the surface area would be the geographic scope of internet access, and the variable element would be the amount of contracted internet bandwidth, which together determine the DDT liability, irrespective of the actual income generated from digital transactions.

The DDT would be designed as a mandatory license-type tax, whose first component would be a toll tax in exchange for internet access to market countries. Depending on the DDT modality, different design options would be available. For example, a global DDT would probably be implemented as a nonrebuttable exclusive tax, which would render it a tax on the amount of contracted internet bandwidth rather than a tax on estimated income, as stated by traditional tax theory. In contrast, national DDTs could allow rebuttable presumptions and establish the DDT as a minimum income tax, which would be compared to the regular income tax that would have been due if the internet user had operated through a permanent establishment in the market jurisdiction. In addition, a global DDT would only be assessed collectively and applied mechanically, while national DDTs would allow for individual determination and discretionary application of the tax.

Hence, the design of national DDTs would be more flexible than the design of a global DDT, while the application and administration of a global DDT would be more restrictive. Both types would be technically feasible, since the technology and information required are fully available; only a proper cooperation framework is missing, which would be solved by creating the GITA and tax collaboration agreements.

Mandatory Registration of a Digital Presence

The introduction of the DDT would be accompanied by a new mandatory registration obligation that would affect all internet users, not only those conducting business, but also those acting as mere customers, viewers, or contributors and irrespective of the geographic location and reach of the internet access and digital interaction of each user. Basically, any individual or entity with a digital presence, understood as a simple internet connection, would have to be registered. This new obligation would build a comprehensive, updated registry of internet users, which would provide valuable information on the internet activities of and interaction between all participants in the digital economy. Additionally, such a user database could be used to educate users on their internet tax obligations and digital responsibility, which would help to advance tax administration practices, especially in B2C and P2P digital transactions, where private internet users could eventually become tax agents and support the tax authorities. Such educational programs would be subsidized and offered by national governments and other specialized agencies, under the guidance of the GITA.

Management of this new digital presence registry would be shared between the GITA and national tax authorities, unless the global DDT is rejected and countries introduce national DDTs unilaterally in an uncoordinated manner. Obviously, the scope of information under each scenario would be different. On the one hand, the GITA would have access to global data from worldwide ISPs, financial institutions,

ICANN, IETF, web-hosting providers, dedicated server hosting providers, and, most important, all member countries' tax authorities. On the other hand, national tax authorities that unilaterally introduce a DDT would only have access to the share of information that concerns their territory, their tax residents, and the nonresidents operating therein; obtaining the data and enforcing the obligation to register would prove time-consuming. From the perspective of internet users, the existence of one global centralized registry, jointly coordinated by the GITA and national tax authorities, would have many benefits. The main benefit would be a drastic reduction in tax compliance costs for users as a result of having to register once worldwide instead of having to register country by country. Furthermore, this global registry would facilitate tax administration, not only of the DDT, but also of any other taxes related to digital transactions (VAT/GST, corporate income tax, personal income tax). For example, national tax authorities could use this information to audit resident taxpayers conducting all or part of their business over the internet (digital business models).

As refers to the registration process, all internet users would be required to submit their tax residence address and national tax identification number (TIN), while business-type users would also be required to provide the IP address and domain name of their websites or the web pages through which they operate online. This information would suffice if the registration process is conducted at a national level for a national DDT. If the registration is coordinated at a global level by the GITA, then each internet user would be assigned a unique internet tax identification number (ITIN) that would serve to identify each internet user across countries under a single identification code for tax purposes. This would be similar to the legal entity identifier (LEI), which is a unique global identifier for legal entities participating in financial transactions.

The newly created ITIN would consolidate information on all internet users from all different sources, including, but not limited to, ISPs, web-hosting services, national tax authorities, and financial entities. To this end, all internet operators would be asked to request and obtain the ITIN from all of their existing and new clients wishing to contract their digital services and carry out financial transactions online. The information should be exchanged automatically among the GITA, the national tax authorities, ISPs, and financial entities, including banks and credit card companies. Member countries would agree to exchange such information upon joining the GITA, while ISPs would be compelled to amend the terms of their standard service contract to include the right to share with the GITA and national tax authorities information on the services provided (contracted internet bandwidth, geographic scope of internet service, IP address, domain name, number and volume of online transactions, number of visits, nature of financial transactions). If needed, contracts would also cover the right to collect the DDT, either as part of their services or through withholdings on financial transactions, when instructed by national tax authorities. In addition, contracts would cover the right to suspend the provision of digital services when required to enforce pending DDT claims and upon official request by the national tax authorities or by the GITA acting by delegation of the national authorities. In practice, such suspension would imply interrupting internet service connection or web-hosting services for internet users that have not complied with their DDT and other tax obligations (tax registration, tax reporting, tax withholding). Finally, simplified registration mechanisms could be established for nonbusiness users or for small and medium internet businesses, based on tax thresholds (amount of contracted internet bandwidth, volume and number of digital transactions), which the GITA would review periodically in consultation with all member countries.

Tax Collection, Enforcement, and Clearinghouse Mechanisms

Collection and enforcement of the DDT would be the most challenging part of administering this new tax, which would vary depending on whether it is applied globally or unilaterally.[4] While unilateral DDTs would differ from each other, which implies the existence of different national DDTs, the global DDT would be a single, uniform levy that would be imposed worldwide and later allocated to member countries that would ultimately have a tax claim over a share of it. Additionally, the global DDT would benefit from the GITA's technical support and coordination, including acting as a clearinghouse for allocating global DDT revenues to all member countries and monitoring tax enforcement tasks across jurisdictions.

Although both national and global DDTs would arise from sovereign taxing rights, their collection and enforcement mechanisms would be significantly different. While unilaterally introduced national DDTs would be administered entirely by each jurisdiction, the global DDT would be administered jointly by the GITA and its member countries, with the assistance of ISPs, web-hosting service providers, and financial entities, which would act as tax agents by collecting the global DDT via withholding.[5] ISPs and web-hosting providers would play a key role in tax collection since these entities would have access to the information needed to assess the global DDT (countries with a digital presence and contracted internet bandwidth). In the subsequent tax allocation process, valuable information on the allocation keys needed to apply the fractional apportionment method (number of digital transactions conducted with each country, number of visits to online websites by country) would be provided by these and other collaborating entities. For example, the International Telecommunication Union, which is the oldest international organization and a UN specialized agency, would be a valuable partner of the GITA, since it is active in broadband internet, internet access, latest-generation wireless technologies, and next-generation networks.

Furthermore, these entities would assist national tax authorities and the GITA in tax enforcement tasks, like facilitating information about their clients' operations within the territory (number of digital transactions conducted with local users, number of local visits to online websites) or suspending the access of noncompliant users to regional or local internet networks and preventing further online business, until pending DDT liabilities are paid, which would apply to both global DDT and national DDT liabilities.

Finally, if DDT is applied unilaterally, DDT revenue collection would belong entirely to the national tax authority, since, as already explained, the tax base of national DDTs incorporates the indicators that are used as allocation keys under the global DDT. If the DDT is applied globally, the GITA could act as a clearinghouse by calculating the share of DDT revenues to be allocated to each country using fractional apportionment on the basis of the allocation keys mentioned. The most efficient scenario would be to have ISPs remit all DDT revenue collected to the GITA; at the end of the fiscal year, the GITA would automatically redistribute and transfer the DDT share allocated to each market jurisdiction. Alternatively, if countries collected DDT revenues, the GITA would compute the DDT transfers necessary to balance DDT collections with the DDT share allocated. Such transfers, either positive or negative, would be made to the GITA, which would redistribute DDT among market jurisdictions, and amounts would be due to the GITA irrespective of actual collections.[6]

Case Study: Global Digital Data Tax Collection and Clearinghouse Mechanisms

This case study illustrates the functioning of the global DDT through tables. It shows how the proposed global DDT and GITA would function, including the information to be collected on GITA member countries, the amount of revenues collected, and the clearinghouse mechanism related to apportioning and distributing the revenues collected (tables 7.1–7.5).

Table 7.1 Information Relevant to a Global Digital Data Tax (by GITA Member Countries)

Country	Digital toll tax	Number of users with SDP	Transactions	Visits
Country A	$500	150,000	20%	40%
Country B	$300	220,000	35%	10%
Country C	$200	70,000	15%	20%
Country D	$800	130,000	25%	5%
Country E	$1,000	180,000	5%	25%
GITA	—	750,000	100%	100%

Source: Original table for this publication.

Note: GITA = global internet tax agency, comprising countries A, B, C, D, and E; SDP = significant digital presence. Number of users may include users with multiple SDPs. Transactions = percentage of global digital transactions conducted with local users. Visits = percentage of global visits from local users.

Table 7.2 Global Digital Data Tax Revenues Collected (by Collaborating Entities)[a]

DDT component	DDT collected
Digital toll tax (country specific)	$439 million
Internet bandwidth tax (global)	$3,750 million

Source: Original table for this publication.

Note: DDT = digital data tax. Assumption: average bandwidth tax per user with significant digital presence = $5,000 per year per market jurisdiction.

a. internet service providers.

Table 7.3 Step 1: Fractional Apportionment (by GITA) of Global Digital Data Tax Collected

Indicator	DDT allocated
Digital toll tax (sum of countries)	$439 million
Allocation key 1: Percentage of transactions	$1,875 million
Allocation key 2: Percentage of visits	$1,875 million

Source: Original table for this publication.
Note: GITA = global internet tax agency; DDT = digital data tax. Assumption: 50% weight of each allocation key for internet bandwidth (component 2). Allocation key 1 = tax proxy for transactions like online marketplaces and digital supplies. Allocation key 2 = tax proxy for online advertising and user-related business models.

Table 7.4 Step 2: Allocation (by Country) of Global Digital Data Tax Collected by GITA

Country	Component 1: digital toll tax	Component 2: internet bandwidth tax		Total DDT allocated
		Allocation key 1	Allocation key 2	
Country A	$75 million	$375 million	$750 million	$1,200 million
Country B	$66 million	$656 million	$188 million	$910 million
Country C	$14 million	$282 million	$375 million	$671 million
Country D	$104 million	$468 million	$94 million	$666 million
Country E	$180 million	$94 million	$468 million	$742 million
GITA	$439 million	$1,875 million	$1,875 million	$4,189 million

Source: Original table for this publication.
Note: GITA = global internet tax agency; DDT = digital data tax. Component 1 = digital toll tax allocated to countries by number of users with a significant digital presence.

Table 7.5 Step 3: Clearinghouse Mechanism (by GITA) of Global Digital Data Tax Allocated

Country	DDT allocated	DDT remitted by ISPs	Balance with GITA
Country A	$1,200 million	$75 + $750 = $825 million	+ $375 million (credit)
Country B	$910 million	$66 + $1,100 = $1,166 million	− $256 million (debit)
Country C	$671 million	$14 + $350 = $364 million	+ $307 million (credit)
Country D	$666 million	$104 + $650 = $754 million	− $88 million (debit)
Country E	$742 million	$180 + $900 = $1,080 million	− $338 million (debit)

Source: Original table for this publication.
Note: GITA = global internet tax agency; DDT = digital data tax; ISP = internet service provider. Assumption: ISPs remit to countries global DDT withheld from users with significant digital presence therein.

Benefits of the Digital Data Tax Proposal

The tax proposal comprises two versions of the new digital data tax, depending on whether it is introduced unilaterally by some jurisdictions in an uncoordinated manner (national DDTs) or is applied jointly by most countries worldwide under the coordination of the global internet tax agency (the global DDT). This section examines the benefits of both types of DDT that recommend their adoption.

Among the common benefits, compliance with tax theory principles is the most fundamental. Both DDT modalities comply with the following tax principles:

- *Horizontal equity principle.* Internet users with a similar digital business presence are taxed alike and vice versa.
- *Benefit principle.* In exchange for paying the DDT, users gain the right to access a digital market and to receive the digital protection of national authorities and the GITA, to the benefit of any internet business operator in new markets.
- *Neutrality principle.* The DDT does not distort investment decisions and can be considered an operating expense and be deductible from residence income taxation, eliminating any disincentive to operate online, including double taxation.
- *Tax sovereignty principle.* The DDT would be levied by national tax authorities.
- *Administrative feasibility principle.* Assessment of the DDT is much simpler than in residual approaches (Amount A).

Therefore, both DDTs are better aligned with traditional tax theory principles than other current tax measures and tax initiatives.

The other important benefit is that the consensual approach required to create the global DDT and the GITA would facilitate the avoidance of double taxation since all member countries would have to agree to provide tax relief, preferably as a tax deduction, for the amount of global DDT paid. Unfortunately, national DDTs would not benefit from this relief, at least at a global scale, and other legal instruments would be required to address this issue. Indeed, the cooperative spirit behind the global DDT would also have an impact on the technical assistance offered to low-tax-capacity countries by the GITA and any other volunteer member countries, which would complement the mission of initiatives like the Platform for Collaboration on Tax. Accordingly, the newly created GITA would act as the global coordinating body on digital taxation and would provide a global forum for countries and organizations worldwide (International Monetary Fund, International Telecommunication Union, OECD, United Nations, World Bank Group, World Trade Organization) to debate on and advance in this area.

Both modalities of the digital data tax, compared to other tax measures like the digital services tax, have several advantages. First, the DDT does not discriminate against entities from specific jurisdictions (China, United States) as a consequence of intended targeting or extremely high revenue thresholds; it applies to all internet users conducting online businesses, irrespective of their turnover or any other threshold. Second, the DDT covers all digital business models, including all tax-disruptive business models, analyzed in chapter 2, preventing any kind of tax discrimination based on the selection of covered services. For example, most digital services taxes and similar taxes focus on taxing only user-related and platform-based tax-disruptive digital business models (online advertising, sale of user-related data, e-commerce marketplaces), while other unilateral taxes (withholding taxes) also cover the supply of digital content (sale, licensing, subscription). However, certain business models are neglected and left outside the scope of application, like regulated online activities (gambling, banking, insurance) and transfers of user-related goodwill. Third, the DDT does not tax nonexistent income as revenue-based taxes do (digital services taxes), because it is a license-type tax that consists of two components, one acting as a toll tax and one acting as a service charge for contracted internet bandwidth (in the global DDT) or for significant digital presence (in national DDTs). Hence, the DDT is consistent with international tax principles and does not unduly increase the tax burden on affected internet users because it constitutes a business operating expense, as already discussed. Lastly, the DDT is not an extra-territorial tax: it only targets online businesses with a significant digital presence in a market country; only businesses that voluntarily decide to conduct online activities therein are subject to paying DDT, which is more of an entrance fee than an income tax. In fact, the DDT resembles a public fee more than a tax, as public fees are satisfied in exchange for a public good or service provided by the government, and the DDT gives access to both the digital market and the digital protection of a market jurisdiction.

Both the global DDT and the GITA would effectively address not only the direct but also the indirect tax challenges of digitalization of the economy in the terms and within the scope of the G-20 mandate. Additionally, this solution would enjoy broad global consensus, since all countries would be invited to join the GITA on a truly equal footing, under the auspices of the United Nations, without giving away any sovereign taxing rights. Instead, the GITA would offer technical support and a global coordination framework to advance digital taxation, to improve tax capacity, and to solve tax disputes, from a fully practicable solution.[7] If the DDT were introduced unilaterally, all of these benefits would also be applicable.

Notes

1. Apart from considerations of tax theory, the DDT would not be a good presumptive income tax because contracted internet bandwidth is not a representative factor of the income ultimately generated by digital companies. For example, some tax-disruptive digital business models may require higher bandwidth capacity (video-streaming services, cloud storage services), but may be less profitable than others that do not need so much internet bandwidth capacity (e-commerce marketplaces, sale and licensing of digital content, online gambling).

2. Professor Hiroshi Kaneko's proposal for an international humanitarian tax, consisting of creating a new personal consumption tax on international airfare, resembles the DDT, since both would be introduced at a national level (Kaneko 1998). However, the revenues raised from the new international humanitarian tax would go into an international fund dedicated to the relief of disaster victims, as opposed to the DDT, which would go into each country's national budget.

3. The DDT would bear no connection to any other taxes, and it would operate as a stand-alone digital license-type tax (not an income tax) that would be independent from the existing GST/VAT indirect tax approach.

4. Some scholars have expressed doubts about how the global version of the DDT would be applied to nonparticipant jurisdictions, if only some countries joined the GITA. In that case, among GITA member countries, the global DDT would be applied, and the GITA would manage the clearinghouse mechanism between its members. However, each of the GITA member countries could opt to apply or not the national version of the DDT to some or all of the nonmember countries worldwide, independently from the GITA.

5. The DDT payment collection function could be made through a "smart contract." The contract would be embedded in the service contract with the ISP (by law), and the funds would transfer automatically on use. This would be a cost of doing internet business, and it could include personal e-mail and social media.

6. The global version of the DDT should be collected in a single currency, to prevent exchange rate and other related issues. The currency should be global, and all internet users, especially DDT taxpayers and tax agents (ISPs) should have access to digital means of exchange: one option could be to use cryptocurrencies to process the DDT payments. However, the choice of cryptocurrency would have to be negotiated. Alternatively, a UN-specific cryptocurrency could be created for DDT purposes. Furthermore, if blockchain technology were to be used, then DDT compliance could be easily monitored globally and remotely, without any need for tax auditors or for costly infrastructure. Obviously, the national version of the DDT would be collected in the national currency, either by ISPs or directly by the local tax administration.

7. All GITA functions would require a strong legal framework, which means that the creation and operations of the GITA would require some form of multilateral convention between all GITA member countries.

Bibliography

Ba, El Hadji Dialigue. 2019. *Le droit fiscal à l´épreuve de la mondialisation: La réglementation des prix de transfert au Sénégal.* Riga: Éditions Universitaires Européennes.

Cordell, Arthur. 1996. "New Taxes for a New Economy." *Government Information in Canada /Information Gouvernementale au Canada* 2 (4): n.p.

Cordell, Arthur. 1997. "Taxing the Internet: The Proposal for a Bit Tax." Speech delivered to the International Tax Program at Harvard Law School, Cambridge, MA, February 14, 1997.

Kaneko, Hiroshi. 1998. "Proposal for International Humanitarian Tax—A Consumption Tax on International Air Travel." *Tax Notes International* 17 (1911): 921–29.

Lucas-Mas, Cristian Óliver. 2002. "The Cuban Tax System through History." *Tax Notes International* 27 (5): 609–30.

Oldman, Oliver, and Elisabeth Owens. 1966. "The International Tax Program." *Canadian Tax Journal* 14: 444.

Tanzi, Vito. 1980. *Potential Income as a Tax Base in Theory and in Practice.* IMF DM/80/84. Washington, DC: International Monetary Fund.

Tanzi, Vito. 1988. "Forces That Shape Tax Policy." In *Tax Policy in the Twenty-First Century,* edited by Herbert Stein. New York: John Wiley and Sons.

Tanzi, Vito. 1999. "Is There a Need for a World Tax Organization?" In *The Economics of Globalization,* edited by Assaf Razin and Efraim Sadka. New York: Cambridge University Press.

Tanzi, Vito. 2001. "Globalization, Technological Development, and the Work of Fiscal Termites." *Brooklyn Journal of International Law* 26 (4): n.p.

Tanzi, Vito. 2016. "Lakes, Oceans, and Taxes: Why the World Needs a World Tax Authority." In *Global Tax Fairness,* edited by Thomas Pogge and Krishen Mehta. Oxford Scholarship Online, March 2016.

UNDP (United Nations Development Programme). 1999. *Human Development Report 1999: Globalization with a Human Face,* ch. 2. New York: Oxford University Press.

Conclusion

The G-20 mandate is clear: to reach a global and consensus-based solution on the tax challenges of the digitalization of the economy. Unfortunately, unilateral taxes and tax initiatives currently under debate do not meet any of the terms of the G-20 mandate. Some exceed the scope (Amount B and Pillar 2 of the Unified Approach of the Organisation for Economic Co-operation and Development [OECD]), while others have limited coverage (digital services taxes, equalization levies), which is a direct consequence of the lack of understanding of what the digital economy is. None is the result of consensual decision making, since some countries have unilaterally introduced tax measures (significant economic presence, digital services taxes), while more than one-third of the international community has not had a say in the main proposal (the Unified Approach) because, to do so, they would have to join the Inclusive Framework on Base Erosion and Profit Shifting (BEPS). Joining the Inclusive Framework requires committing to implementing the four minimum standards, which have nothing to do with taxation of the digital economy. Lastly, for current options to be truly global, political buy-in by national stakeholders worldwide would be required to guarantee an effective and global implementation of the solution. Such buy-in is very improbable without a forum that brings together all countries—even more so, given the clash of national economic interests, where market jurisdictions claim new taxing rights at the expense of eroding the tax bases of residence countries.

As analyzed in this book, market jurisdictions' tax aspirations are unsubstantiated and contravene the most basic traditional tax theory principles, giving rise to a series of legal, economic, tax policy, and tax administration issues that policy makers cannot overlook. Ultimately, they must devise a solution that the global community can support, which requires meeting some minimum standards in terms of scope, tax fairness, nondiscrimination, administrative feasibility, and tax sovereignty. Otherwise, the solution will fail. Sadly, nowadays, many governments are in great need of additional sources of tax revenue. Rather than incurring the political cost of raising taxes on their citizens, they opt for claiming new taxing rights over foreign businesses, even if the ultimate tax burden will surely be shifted to and borne by their own citizens. This approach raises serious concerns, not only from the perspective of traditional tax theory, but also from the standpoint of tax sovereignty, since market jurisdictions are trying to alleviate their fiscal deficits by overburdening foreign online businesses, generating double taxation, harming competitiveness, and discouraging digital entrepreneurship. This is not tax competition, but a totally different ball game, where countries are willing to undermine the very foundations of the international tax order and to invade and usurp sovereign taxing rights in order to cover up the deficiencies of their failed domestic fiscal policies.

In fairness, no country should dip into other countries' efforts, which is exactly what market jurisdictions aim to do when claiming new taxing rights outside the framework of traditional tax theory. Indeed, countries where technological companies are resident have been supporting, promoting, and investing in research, development, and innovation for decades, which obviously has a significant economic cost for such countries in the form of tax incentives, public subsidies, tax credits and deductions, or loss write-offs. Banks and venture capitalists also bear significant costs because they provide funding via debt or equity for high-risk investments, since just a handful of start-ups bloom and even fewer become profitable. Ultimately, failed internet ventures affect their countries' economies, which absorb bad debts from banks and capital losses from investors and even bail out the financial sector and failed industries when economic downturns occur.

Therefore, market countries cannot expect to share only in gains and not in losses, which is exactly what these new tax claims aspire to do. Interestingly enough, unilateral taxes (digital services taxes, equalization levies) do not tax profits; instead, they tax specified services on a gross basis, which may result in taxation of nonexistent profits. Such tax measures are only addressed to share in gains, even if no gains exist. Understandably, internet companies and their countries of tax residence are reluctant to accept new taxing rights that disrupt the tax status quo on which the international tax order is based and functions. If internet businesses were also to be taxed from now on by market jurisdictions and no tax relief were provided, the consequences would be extremely damaging to the global economy, since companies would shift whenever possible the additional tax burden from double taxation to their customers worldwide. Alternatively, if they were to absorb this additional tax cost, their profitability would be drastically reduced, which would increase their cost of capital as a result of their increased business risk and lower rates of return. Such a situation would cause adverse economic effects at a global scale.

Although we started the tax technical analysis of this book without any preconceived ideas, we found ourselves with a very straightforward conclusion: traditional tax theory does not support income taxation of remote digital suppliers by source jurisdictions. Aware of market countries' need to raise revenue from the digital economy, we decided to explore alternative untaxed digital transactions that could increase their fiscal space.

We came up with the international supply of internet bandwidth to access digital markets, which is the digital transaction that our digital data tax (DDT) would tax. The proposed DDT is a license-type consumption tax, rather than an income tax. It is aligned with tax principles and, as a consequence, does not conflict with any other income tax proposals (OECD's Unified Approach). It aims to tax different transactions from the opposite tax perspective: our DDT proposal taxes foreign digital companies as consumers, while income tax proposals tax them as suppliers.

Finally, our proposal involves the creation of a global internet tax agency (GITA) in which all countries may participate as equals. This agency would bring together the entire global community and provide a neutral forum for political discussion and technical assistance in the area of digital taxation. The digital economy is a global phenomenon that requires a global solution: the creation of global taxing mechanisms and global institutions that provide technical assistance and support for successful global implementation.

ECO-AUDIT

Environmental Benefits Statement

The World Bank Group is committed to reducing its environmental footprint. In support of this commitment, we leverage electronic publishing options and print-on-demand technology, which is located in regional hubs worldwide. Together, these initiatives enable print runs to be lowered and shipping distances decreased, resulting in reduced paper consumption, chemical use, greenhouse gas emissions, and waste.

We follow the recommended standards for paper use set by the Green Press Initiative. The majority of our books are printed on Forest Stewardship Council (FSC)–certified paper, with nearly all containing 50–100 percent recycled content. The recycled fiber in our book paper is either unbleached or bleached using totally chlorine–free (TCF), processed chlorine–free (PCF), or enhanced elemental chlorine–free (EECF) processes.

More information about the Bank's environmental philosophy can be found at http://www.worldbank.org/corporateresponsibility.